Praise for **Ready** FOR **Kindergarten!**

"As an early childhood professional, I look to Deborah as a resource when I am doing curriculum planning and searching for creative and practical ideas that support young children's development. *Ready for Kindergarten!* provides specific ideas that parents and caregivers can use right away with the children in their care. Each area of development is covered with tips that are clear, intentional, and support hands-on exploration for our youngest learners. This book is a 'must have' for our teacher library!"

—Laura Eldredge, co-founder of The SEEDS Network, LLC
(*www.theseedsnetwork.com*)

"Covering everything from selecting a backpack to bathroom independence, Deborah hits it out of the park with *Ready for Kindergarten!* Parents will devour this easy-to-read guide that is sure to both settle nerves and assure readiness. I was amazed at both the level of detail and simple, easy-to-read format of Deborah's book. As a kindergarten teacher, I can only hope the parents of my future students read this book and take her advice to heart."

—Matt Halpern, kindergarten teacher and creator of
LookAtMyHappyRainbow.com

Ready FOR Kindergarten!

From Recognizing Colors
to Making Friends,
Your Essential Guide
to Kindergarten Prep

DEBORAH J. STEWART, MEd

Avon, Massachusetts

Published by
Adams Media, a division of F+W Media, Inc.
57 Littlefield Street, Avon, MA 02322. U.S.A.
www.adamsmedia.com

ISBN 10: 1-4405-6523-6
ISBN 13: 978-1-4405-6523-6
eISBN 10: 1-4405-6524-4
eISBN 13: 978-1-4405-6524-3

Printed in the United States of America.

10 9 8 7 6 5 4 3 2 1

Cover image © 123rf.com/Bartlomiej Jaworski.

*This book is available at quantity discounts for bulk purchases.
For information, please call 1-800-289-0963.*

DEDICATION

This book is dedicated to my two grandsons, Kai and Xander, who will soon be heading off to enjoy their own kindergarten experience. It is my hope that their journey from early childhood to kindergarten and beyond is filled with exceptionally rewarding experiences every step of the way.

Contents

Introduction

The early childhood years are an amazing time of growth and development, and each stage of life is just as important as the next when it comes to helping young children prepare for success in kindergarten. The kinds of playful and nurturing experiences offered by parents and caregivers play an important role in helping young children reach their greatest potential during these critical years of development. Whether it is a brand new baby bouncing on daddy's knee, or a toddler dumping blocks all over the floor, or a three-year-old getting hands messy with paint, you should celebrate each stage of a young child's life and consider each equally important in the process of preparing for kindergarten.

Throughout this book, you will find simple to read and apply tips on what you can do to build on the foundations that you have nurtured throughout early childhood. As you help your child prepare for success in school, those foundations are now ready for a little polishing. Reading along, you may recognize many of the skills as ones your child is already starting to exhibit. This book will help you recognize the significance of these skills in preparing for kindergarten so that you can continue to offer your child new opportunities to master them.

Each section of this book is broken down into small, easy to read and understand pieces of information that include the following:

1. **WHAT YOUR CHILD SHOULD KNOW:** In this section, you will be given an overview of the developmental skills your child should have a good grasp of before heading off to kindergarten.
2. **HOW YOU CAN HELP:** In this section, I'll give you tips and suggestions on how you can help your child master the developmental skills.
3. **REVIEW, REVISE, REVISIT:** In this section, we'll discuss simple ways you can figure out how your child is doing. Keep in mind that learning comes through building on prior knowledge and experiences. As you review your child's progress, you will want to revise your plans and activities to fit your child's interests and abilities. Then revisit the activities to give your child additional opportunities to build new knowledge and to develop new skills.

Since many of the skills being highlighted throughout the book happen simultaneously as a child develops, it is best to read the book in its entirety first. Then go back and review the helpful tips as needed. *Ready for Kindergarten!* is based on the belief that parents play an important role in their child's education, and that there is always the need for a little guidance and support along the way. The book is rich with ideas and will be the kind of resource you can come back and review all throughout your child's prekindergarten year.

Ready for Kindergarten! is written with the assumption that you, as a parent or caregiver, recognize that each stage of growth and development is equally important and that you have worked diligently to invite your toddler to be a toddler and your three-year-old to be a three-year-old. While picking up another basket of dumped toys or wiping finger paint off tiny fingers, you instinctively know that these kinds of experiences are an important part of a child's development and are a part of the building blocks that lead your child to success in kindergarten.

However, within a year of your child's heading off to kindergarten, you can start to look back and worry whether you have done enough to help him be prepared for that next big step. *Ready for Kindergarten!* is written specifically for the parents and caregivers of children who are within that final year of preparation. It's a big step . . . but it's also the next stage on a wonderful journey that you and your child will take together.

PART I

Building Strength from Fingers to Toes

The kinds of physical growth that take place during the first five years of life are remarkable, but now that your child is getting ready for kindergarten, you will naturally start to take a closer look at the finer details of his physical abilities. Perhaps you notice that your child struggles with the strength to hold a writing tool firmly or lacks the coordination to cut with a pair of scissors. Perhaps you realize that you are always zipping up your child's coat or carrying his bags in from the car. And perhaps you remember that it's been awhile since you went outside to toss a ball or fly a kite with him.

Fine-motor skills, large-motor skills, and self-help skills are all examples of physical readiness. They take time, patience, and opportunity to develop fully but all are essential components of kindergarten success. As you integrate a broad range of physical skills into everyday meaningful and playful experiences, your child will begin to develop the strength, balance, coordination, and confidence he needs to be physically ready for kindergarten.

CHAPTER 1

I Can Do It Myself

Part of preparing for success in kindergarten is mastering self-help skills. These can include anything from washing hands to organizing a backpack. As your child builds his own collection of self-help skills, he will be less dependent on others to get through the fundamentals of a classroom day. Let's take a look at some of the basic skills and processes your child should have a good grasp of in preparation for success in kindergarten.

SCRUB-A-DUB-DUB

Hand washing may seem like a simple process that any child should be able to do, but often we take for granted the most basic self-help skills and never really think them through. Hand washing is something your child will be doing daily, so, at the very least, the skill is worth a few minutes of your time to make sure your child's process is going well.

What Your Child Should Know

Hand washing comes with a complete set of skills including:

▶ Having a pretty good grasp of which sink handle is for cold water and which is for warm water

▶ Knowing how to turn the water on and off

▶ Having some sense of how much soap is needed for one hand-washing session and how to operate a soap dispenser

▶ Knowing how to rub hands together to wash the germs away

▶ Understanding how to rinse hands completely

▶ Knowing how to use one (or two at the most) paper towel for drying hands or how to operate a hand-drying machine

▶ Knowing how to throw used paper towels in the trash, rather than leaving them by the sink or tossing them on the floor

How You Can Help

When it comes to helping master the process of washing hands, consider providing a little parallel hand-washing guidance. Have your child wash her hands along with you so you can model the process. If you have a double sink, parallel hand washing can really work well, but even with a single sink, modeling the hand-washing process can be a very effective way to help your child understand what she needs to do.

▶ Set up a hand-washing center by setting out a basket of paper towels, a soap dispenser, and a trash can near your sink.

▶ Use a little self-talk (that is, talk out loud to yourself about what you are doing as you go through the process). "First I need to turn on the water." "Next I need to put one pump of soap on my hand." "Now I need to rub my hands together." "It's time to rinse off the soap," and so on.

▶ As you model and self-talk through the process, invite your child to wash her hands beside you.

If your child is having trouble knowing the difference between the hot and cold water handles, consider wrapping a red rubber band around your hot water handle and a blue rubber band around your cold water handle. This will help your child notice the difference between the two handles and think about which temperature of water is adjusted by which handle. Additional reading: Handwashing Fun! (*www.amomwithalessonplan.com/childrens-mucinex*).

Reflect, Revise, Revisit

While you are walking through the hand-washing process, you will be able to identify areas that your child doesn't seem to grasp or has a tendency to skip over.

Don't turn an individual hand-washing session into a major ordeal; the object here isn't to get it absolutely right the first time. Instead, have several mini-sessions until your child seems to know what comes next naturally. Remind your child regularly to wash his hands after play, before eating, and after going to the bathroom, using the same process each time. Developing a healthy and simple hand-washing routine at home will lead toward healthy habits in the kindergarten classroom, too!

POTTY BREAK

Hopefully, by the time your child is headed off to kindergarten, he will be fully independent when it comes to going to the bathroom. However, potty breaks involve many skills in which your child will need to feel confident.

What Your Child Should Know

By the time your child is ready to head off to the kindergarten classroom he should know skills, including:

▶ Knowing the difference between the "boys" and "girls" bathroom labels commonly seen on most public bathroom doors

▶ Being able to go to the correct bathroom

▶ Remembering to shut the door

▶ Knowing how to take off the necessary clothing

▶ Knowing how to use the bathroom

▶ Pulling off a reasonable amount of toilet paper from the roll

▶ Being able to wipe his own bottom

▶ Flushing the toilet

▶ Putting the necessary clothing back on

▶ Washing his hands before leaving the bathroom

How You Can Help

Potty training is a process that begins at a very early age for most children, so by the time they are ready to enter kindergarten they probably know most of the skills needed to be independent. However, there are two skills that can still present quite a challenge. The first is the ability to undress and dress oneself. You can help your child by making sure he can manage the clothing of choice. Pay attention to which type of clothing is creating stumbling blocks towards independence and take the time to help manage the problem area (buttons, zippers, tights, or belts) until he's got it. If you see your child still struggling with clothing, consider sending him to school in clothing that he can easily manage independently and continue to work at home on the clothing that he still needs to master.

The second top issue in the potty process is wiping her own bottom. At home, a child may feel comfortable asking for help with the wiping process, but at school this sort of request will probably strike your child as awkward. Furthermore, as a general rule, kindergarten teachers prefer not to wipe their students' bottoms. Help build the confidence and skills needed to be completely independent in the potty process. If he needs more practice wiping his own bottom, then take the time and patience to practice this process consistently. Break the process down into steps if needed, but don't make bottom wiping a frustrating experience. Instead, help your child feel a sense of accomplishment and develop the confidence to complete the potty process without your assistance. You might have to put up with yucky underpants for a few days, but better to have an extra load of laundry than a child who is regularly dependent on others.

Reflect, Revise, Revisit

Be aware of how long your child is taking in the bathroom at home or when going out to public places and be curious as to why. If he's in and out in less than a minute, chances are he might have forgotten to wash his hands. If your child is in the potty for an hour, chances are that either he has a very bad tummy ache or he is using potty time as play time. In either case, just make yourself aware of how he's using his time in the bathroom and whether there is a need for you to explain the process and the rules of using the bathroom a little more clearly.

IT'S TIME TO EAT!

Chances are your child will be eating a snack, and possibly lunch as well, in kindergarten. Of course, most kindergarten-age children know how to eat their food, but there are some skills that may need a little extra attention in order to help the eating process run smoothly.

What Your Child Should Know

The eating skills your child should know include:

► Knowing what kinds of meals or snacks she will be eating

► Knowing what time of day she will be eating at school

► Knowing how to manage any food items brought to school for snack or lunch in a lunch box or bag

► Knowing how to open a lunch box or container

► Knowing how to sit at the table and eat in a timely manner

The reality is, most kindergarten classrooms have a limited amount of time for snacks or lunch and getting the most of their eating times will require your child to be able to sit down and focus on eating rather than using that time for play.

How You Can Help

The timing of snacks and lunches in kindergarten is important. For example, will snack time be right after morning circle and will lunchtime be right after reading time? For some kindergarten-age children, not knowing when snack or lunchtime is can be a huge distraction to their ability to focus. Having a sense of when lunch or snack time will fall during the school day can help your child mentally and physically deal with how long it will be before it is time to eat.

Just before kindergarten begins, see if your child's teacher can provide you with a daily schedule. Talk about the schedule with your child and help him visualize the order of the day. Perhaps even make a poster with pictures to help define the daily schedule so your child has a good grasp of when snack or lunchtime will fall.

To help your child adjust to the eating schedule, you might consider matching the eating schedule at home for a few days or weeks. This will help your child get used to the eating schedule and avoid a big jolt in the transition from home to school.

Have lunch box meals at home so your child can get into the practice of opening and eating from one. Invite him to carry the lunch box to the table, open it up, and select the foods to eat, then put the contents back inside, and close the box.

Continue to help your child strengthen fine-motor skills by inviting him to open food containers and packages. Sometimes, the ability to open containers requires hand or finger strength, and sometimes it's as simple as showing your child where to find the dotted line on a package or how to pull a tab properly. Look for tips and tricks you can teach to open food and drink containers.

Reflect, Revise, Revisit

Give ample opportunity to be as independent as possible during meal times. Have lunch box meals and use them to reflect on your child's eating habits and skills. Sitting and eating together during lunch or snack will help you gauge what your child is struggling with and whether or not you need to give tips to help him open a container or reminders to help her stay focused on eating. Remember to keep the experience of eating together simple, positive, and fun.

Having a lunch box meal with your child will also help you gauge what types of food it's reasonable for your child to eat in a short time. It may be necessary for you to cut back and not send quite as much food or to simplify the way you pack the food.

Be prepared for your child to come home hungry after school for quite some time. Even with all the preparations you provide, he'll still find his new schedule and eating lunch with friends at school to be an adjustment and most likely will have a hungry tummy when getting home.

JACKETS AND COATS, OH MY!

In a full classroom of children, taking the time to help each child put on a jacket or coat can eat up valuable time for play and learning. It is a very good idea to help your child develop his ability to put on his own jacket or coat.

What Your Child Should Know

Your child should know how to put on his own jacket, but this is only part of that process. Other things include:

▶ Knowing how to take off the jacket without turning either sleeve wrong side out

▶ Knowing how to recognize when a sleeve is turned wrong side out and how to straighten it back up

▶ Knowing where to stash mittens and hats

How You Can Help

One way to teach a young child how to put on his own coat or jacket is by following these basic steps:

1. Lay the coat on the floor with the zipper or opening side of the coat facing up and open so you can see where the inside of the armholes are.

2. Invite your child to stand with the hood or the neck of the coat between or in front of his feet. He should be standing at the head of the jacket looking down with the rest of the coat stretched out in front.
3. Next, show your child how to reach down and slide his hands inside the armholes of the coat.
4. Now he should lift up the coat with both hands in the armholes and slide the coat over his head while at the same time sliding both hands all the way to the ends of each sleeve. Additional reading: How to Put a Coat On (*www .teachpreschool.org/2013/02/how-to-put-on-a-coat*).

Mastering the ability to put on a coat or jacket is the best place to start. Once your child has learned the process of putting on his own coat, then you can begin teaching how to zip up zippers or put on mittens and scarves, but good coat management is always the top priority.

Often, if children get into the habit of tucking mittens or hats into a pocket or the sleeve of their coats, they'll do a good job of taking inventory of their belongings and tracking where everything is. This is a useful habit to practice, perhaps after you've been out for a walk together and are taking off your coats.

Reflect, Revisit, Revise

The best way see how well the process of putting on coats is going is by recognizing how often you step in and help your child compared to how often your child completes the process on his own. Observe and give tips, if needed, along the way.

Keep in mind that it may just be a matter of time and practice before your child will develop the coordination needed.

If your child continues to struggle putting on his own coat, make sure that the coat isn't too thick or doesn't have too many buttons. Perhaps try teaching the process with a lighter jacket; when your child has the process down, try it with a heavier coat. Remember that a coat with lots of zippers, buttons, or other bells and whistles just might be too cool for school!

BACKPACK SAVVY

When the start of kindergarten is just around the corner, you may find yourself with a long list of school supplies to buy. One of those items may very well be a new backpack. Of course, your child will pick out the coolest backpack ever made and be excited to rush home and fill it up. However, before jumping too far ahead, consider slowing down and making sure your child is backpack savvy.

What Your Child Should Know

Your child should know a few things about her backpack, such as:

► Knowing how the backpack opens and closes

► Knowing what is supposed to go into the backpack before school

▶ Knowing what is supposed to go into the backpack after school

▶ Knowing where things like paper, pencils, folders, lunch money, notes to the teacher, and other things belong in the backpack

▶ Knowing where the backpack goes when at home so it is easy to find for the next day

▶ Knowing how to carry a backpack

Oh yes, an entire tutorial may be necessary along with a little practice so your child will confidently know how to organize, manage, carry, and take care of her own backpack.

How You Can Help

Before filling up your child's backpack with all the goodies on your school supply list, take time to divide up the items by what will stay in her backpack versus items that won't. Place the items that won't stay in the backpack in a separate bag with a note attached titled "Mary's School Supplies." Then invite your child to help you put the items that she'll need every day inside the backpack. Once everything is neatly in the backpack, invite your child to:

▶ Put the backpack on

▶ Walk around the room with the backpack on

▶ Walk between a few tight spaces with the backpack on

▶ Take the backpack off

▶ Open the backpack

▶ Take a few items out of the backpack and put them all back in

▶ Close the backpack

▶ Hang the backpack up on a hook

▶ Find where you have boldly printed her name on the backpack (just in case someone else happened to pick the same cool backpack)

Reflect, Revise, Revisit

Start by deciding whether or not the backpack you and your child chose is, in fact, the right choice: Is there a special pocket for pencils? Will her take-home folder fit easily inside the backpack? Are there too many pockets or not enough pockets? Is the backpack too heavy? Can your child slip the backpack on and off her back without any help? Can she easily open and close it?

Your child may need some practice to master the skills of backpack management, so don't expect perfection, but do make sure the backpack you have selected will help your child successfully carry her things to and from school.

CHAPTER 2

Fine-Motor Skills

Behind every successful attempt at learning to write, cut, draw, lace a shoe, button a shirt, zip up a jacket—and the list goes on—are strong fine-motor skills. Each of the following tasks will help your child begin to build and strengthen these abilities. This chapter will introduce the tools commonly used in the kindergarten classroom and show you ways to promote the fine-motor skills needed to manipulate each of them.

CUTTING WITH SCISSORS

It is most likely that you will find scissors on the "back-to-school" shopping list. You will want to select a good pair of child-sized scissors that your child can hold comfortably in his hand and that will easily cut paper. Be leery of really cheap scissors as these can make the cutting process more difficult and they will most likely fall apart before too long. If your child is still zigzagging back and forth between using his left versus right hand, then you might look for a pair of scissors that can be used in either hand or buy two different pairs of scissors—one left-handed and one right-handed pair. It is not recommended that you force your child to choose which hand must be used for cutting. Instead provide the tools your child will need as he figures out what works best.

What Your Child Should Know

The skills involving the safe and creative use of scissors, including:

► Knowing how to hold a pair of scissors properly with his hands and fingers

► Being able to open and close the scissors using one hand

► Being able to cut a variety of different types of materials

► Knowing how to carry scissors safely from one location to another

How You Can Help

Provide your child with many different types of materials to practice cutting. Some of the materials you may set out with a pair of scissors include: Play-Doh, paper, newspaper, magazines, cards, ribbon, lace, fabric, straws, grass, and other interesting materials. You want to keep the development of fine-motor skills interesting and open-ended so your child's focus stays on investigating the process rather than always getting it right.

As your child becomes more proficient at managing and manipulating the scissors, you may want to provide paper with lines for your child to try to cut along. Don't rush into structuring your child's cutting experiences and mastery. Allow ample time for him to build his cutting skills so that he will feel competent and confident in the cutting process.

Reflect, Revise, Revisit

While your child is exploring how to cut different materials, observe how he's holding the scissors and which hand he tends to use the most when cutting. If he continues to struggle with holding the scissors correctly after he's had ample time and opportunity, then investigate the problem a bit. Do you need to buy a different type of scissors? Are you giving your child plenty of opportunities and time to explore the process of cutting?

Remember, learning how to cut can be integrated with many other skills and activities, and mastery of this skill takes time. Keep it fun and turn the pressure off so your child will successfully reach his potential and maintain a sense of confidence along the way. Additional reading: Cutting with Scissors (*www.msbarbarasblog.blogspot.com/2012/09/pre school-cutting-with-scissors.html*).

WRITING TOOLS

In learning to write, your child first needs time to explore a variety of writing tools. Over time you will introduce how to hold writing tools properly and your child will begin to perfect her skills in using those tools. For now, the goal is to introduce a variety of writing tools and give your child opportunities to explore those tools as a way to promote her fine-motor strength and skills.

What Your Child Should Know

Writing is an essential part of the school curriculum. At this stage, the skills your child will learn include:

▶ Recognizing and naming different types of writing tools

▶ Having a good grasp on how to manipulate and work with all types of writing tools

▶ Knowing how to care for and organize her writing tools

▶ Knowing how to sharpen a pencil, put lids back on markers, and put crayons back into the box

How You Can Help

Prepare a writing center: This is a place your child can go to color, draw, write, and explore different types of writing tools and paper. A writing center can be a specific table and shelf or it can be a box that you keep filled with your child's writing tools. Keep the writing center creative and accessible so your child will find exploring the writing process fun and interesting.

Add a variety of writing tools to your child's writing center such as crayons, thin markers, thick markers, pencils, colored pencils, and so on. It isn't necessary to put every type of writing tool you have out at one time. You may want to rotate items so the writing center stays fresh and interesting.

Include different kinds of paper and a clipboard or notebook to promote more interest in writing. Include envelopes, stickers, stamps, and other items that your child can integrate into the writing process and that will promote creative thinking. Add a few envelopes and your child may wish to pretend her writing center is a post office where she can write letters. Add a clipboard and your child may pretend to write up orders or lists.

Continue to rotate different tools and materials that will promote your child's joy in the writing experience and invite her to continue building her fine-motor strength and skills needed for future handwriting success. For more ideas, see this Writing Center from Pre-K Pages (*www.pre-kpages.com/writing_center/*).

Reflect, Revise, Revisit

As your child spends time at the writing center, take notice of her choices in writing tools and which tools she avoids. Do a little investigating to find out why she might not enjoy a specific tool. Is it broken? Does it need to be sharpened? Does your child not know how to use it effectively? See what you can do to help.

If your child isn't showing any interest in the writing center, you may need to be more involved. It is always more fun when two people interact with each other. You can role-play together or simply sit down to color and draw together. Writing shouldn't feel isolating and lonely. Rather, it can be a rich environment and experience you both can enjoy together.

SEWING AND WEAVING

Another fun way to invite creativity and to build fine-motor skills is to invite your child to try his hand at sewing and weaving. Don't think that this is a process only interesting to girls. Boys are also capable at sewing and weaving, and it will be a valuable skill for learning to lace a shoe or tie a knot in the future.

What Your Child Should Know

Your child should know how to thread sewing and weaving materials in and out of a variety of canvasses.

How You Can Help

Put together a sewing box for your child. His sewing box might include plastic needles, different types of yarn, ribbon, thread, and lace. Show him how to keep his sewing box organized and switch out the sewing tools in the box on occasion to keep the process inviting and fresh.

Now that the sewing box is ready to go, you will need to be on the lookout for different sewing and weaving materials your child can use with the tools. Here are a few fun and creative sewing and weaving ideas you can share with him:

▶ Anything with holes in it such as a strawberry basket or a paper plate with holes punched around the edge can be a fun weaving canvas. Your child can weave ribbon through the strawberry basket or yarn through the holes of the paper plate.

▶ Try weaving on a grander scale. Give your child crepe paper to weave in and out of furniture around the house, then crawl through it like an obstacle course, or take yarn outdoors to weave around trees to climb over and under.

▶ Materials such as plastic mesh provide a sturdy canvas for sewing, and your child can thread a plastic needle through a set of cut up straws, large pasta, or buttons with big holes.

To continue your child's interest in the weaving and sewing process, be on the lookout for other interesting objects and materials that change up the type of weaving and sewing he can explore. Additional reading: Sewing

Frame for Preschoolers (*www.teachpreschool.org/2012/02/ diy-sewing-frame-for-preschoolers*) and Weaving Through a Rainbow (*www.teachpreschool.org/2013/03/ weaving-through-a-rainbow*).

Reflect, Revise, Revisit

As you share different sewing and weaving processes with your child, be observant of his ability to thread the needle or keep the string from getting tangled up. Evaluate where he needs assistance and show him tips to keep the process from getting frustrating. Your child's fine-motor development will benefit greatly from practicing sewing and weaving skills. You want to make sure you help to keep the process manageable so he'll have a successful experience.

TWISTING AND TURNING

Twisting and turning is a wonderful way to strengthen the muscles in the hands and wrist. As your child's hands and wrists continue to be strengthened she will be able to have a firmer grip on tools and materials commonly used in the kindergarten classroom.

What Your Child Should Know

Your child should know how to accomplish basic everyday tasks, including:

▶ Opening a lid

▶ Turning a water faucet off and on

▶ Squeezing out a wet washrag

The more your child can accomplish these tasks without your help, the more she will strengthen and build fine-motor skills as well as prepare to take care of her own needs in kindergarten.

How You Can Help

The next time you are preparing to open a container for your child, stop and consider if this is something she could do on her own. It is easy to take everyday tasks for granted and just do them, but you want to foster her independence. As well, you're helping her build those important muscles in her hands and fingers. Here are a few fun ideas to give your child's wrist and hands a little exercise:

▶ Set out some keys and locks and invite your child to match the keys to the locks and then try to open them.

▶ Try a little wrist twist art. Place two or three drops of colorful paint in the center of a sheet of heavy paper, then invite your child to place a paper plate, paper cup, or a lid from a jar on top of the paint. Now firmly hold the chosen object with the entire hand and press down firmly and twist the object to mix the colors of paint together. After giving a few twists, lift up the object and see the twisted design. Add more paint and try it again! Additional reading: Paper Plate Spin Art (*www.teachpreschool.org/2011/04/ paper-plate-spin-art-without-the-spinner-for-preschoolers*).

▶ Place several sizes and types of empty plastic bottles on the table and invite your child to fill them up with water and then put the lid back on. Bring the filled bottles over to a sink and see if the lids are on tight enough by turning them upside down over the sink. Did the water stay in the bottles or did it come gushing out? Discuss what happened with your child and why and what can be done to fix any problems that might have occurred.

▶ There are lots of opportunities for twisting and turning in the kitchen, from turning the handle on a salad spinner to whipping up cookie mix with a big spoon. If you happen to have a few nonelectronic kitchen tools like a handheld can opener or old-fashioned egg beater, these make wonderful tools for exercising those wrists and hands, too!

Reflect, Revise, Revisit

Twisting and turning involves both fine-motor strength and coordination, which can lead most adults to opening lids and turning handles for their child. Instead, get in the practice of giving your child part of the responsibility to help build those twisting and turning skills.

TWEEZING AND SPOONING

Your child most certainly knows how to use a spoon by now, but a pair of tweezers might be a new experience for her. Tweezing and spooning are processes that involve concentration and eye-hand coordination.

What Your Child Should Know

Your child should be able to concentrate on tasks that involve small objects and fine details. As she spends time tweezing and spooning, she will be building her ability to concentrate, which is a very important part of kindergarten success.

How You Can Help

Tweezing involves using different types of tweezers, chopsticks, and tongs to pick up objects and move them from one location to another. The smaller the objects, the more your child will need to concentrate on picking the objects up and placing them in the desired location.

Set out an empty egg carton, twelve buttons in a bowl, and tweezers. Invite your child to pick up one button at a time with the tweezers and then place each button in one of the egg carton cups. You can change up the materials, but the process should remain the same. For example, instead of tweezers use tongs, instead of buttons use pom-poms, and instead of an egg carton use cups.

Spooning is a similar process to tweezing, only instead of using tweezers, your child must use a spoon to move objects from one place to another. Change the size of the spoons, objects, and containers.

For both spooning and tweezing, change the distance between containers. For example, can your child pick up a ball with only a spoon and then walk it all the way across the room to drop it in a basket?

Reflect, Revise, Revisit

Keep the process of spooning and tweezing interesting and fun and as you observe your child try each process, consider how you can make it more challenging. If your child is getting frustrated or bored with a process, consider how you can change things up. Try a little spooning up Ping-Pong balls from a tub of water or tweezing the seeds out of the center of an apple. The goal is to build up concentration, not to get frustrated and quit. Find the right types of challenges and increase them over time. Additional reading: I Wonder What Is Inside a Gourd? (*www.teachpreschool.org/2012/10/ scientific-discoveries-I-wonder-what-is-in-inside-a-gourd/*).

SCOOPING AND POURING

There are many opportunities to get your child involved in scooping and pouring that help to build independence and also serve to strengthen hands and wrists.

What Your Child Should Know

Scooping and pouring are great activities for building fine-motor skills. These are also skills that require practice and patience. Among the skills your child will develop are:

▶ The ability to pour his own cup of juice and scoop up his own Teddy Grahams with a measuring cup at snack time.

▶ The skills to create and build with different materials such as scooping up sand in a bucket, packing it down, and dumping it over to make a sand castle.

▶ The ability to dig a hole to plant flowers and to fill up a watering can to give his flowers a drink of water.

How You Can Help

Give your child ample time in play with scoops, pitchers, shovels, buckets, and cups. Here a few ideas that you can invite your child to explore:

▶ Water play is always fun for young children, and there are many places you can set up a little water play area for your child. Set up a small tub of water on a towel on the kitchen floor. Take water play outdoors on the back porch. Add tools for play in the bathtub.

▶ Let your child help you wash the dishes and then stick around for a little extra water play in the kitchen sink. Add a few cups, pitchers, funnels, and scoops and let your child explore scooping and pouring water.

▶ Sand play is another fun way to promote scooping and pouring. You may prefer to keep sand play outdoors, but just like water play, add different tools that invite scooping and pouring.

▶ Cooking is filled with lots of scooping and pouring and involves concentration, math skills, as well as science. Whether your child invents his own recipes out of a little flour, sugar, and spice or whips up a real recipe with you for the entire family to enjoy, get your child scooping, measuring, pouring, stirring, and cooking.

Reflect, Revise, Revisit

The possibilities for integrating fine-motor skill development into a cooking, math, science, or daily-life skill lesson are endless. As you observe your child's scooping and pouring, build on his skills by letting him serve his own snack or take personal responsibility for watering his own plant. As your child participates in these experiences, you will be able to observe and help your child think about things like how much water is too much water. Over time, your child will begin to master the processes involving scooping and pouring. Additional reading: Everyday Sensory Play in Preschool (*www.teachpreschool.org/2011/11/everyday-sensory-play-in-preschool/*).

PLAY-DOUGH

Play-dough is an exceptional material for promoting fine-motor strength and skills. There are many different recipes for making homemade play-dough, and this is one of the most common recipes you can try.

You Will Need:

1 cup flour
¼ cup salt
2 teaspoons cream of tartar
1 tablespoon vegetable oil
1 cup water
Food coloring (optional)

► Mix the flour, salt, and cream of tartar in a pot.

► Add the oil and water and cook the mixture over a medium heat, stirring constantly, until the mixture starts to thicken and becomes a soft and pliable (play-dough like) ball.

► Remove the play-dough from the pot and place the dough on a tray or sheet of wax paper. Continue to knead the dough until it cools; your play-dough is now ready.

► Optional: Add a few drops of food color to the water before cooking to change the color of the dough. Add a touch of scented oil or seasoning to give your play-dough a fun smell. Add seeds or glitter to give your dough an interesting texture.

What Your Child Should Know

Play-dough can teach many important skills, including:

▶ How to manipulate play-dough into different forms such as a ball or a snake

▶ How to combine the use of play-dough with other skills such as cutting, squeezing, pulling, pinching, and rolling

How You Can Help

Give your child plenty of opportunities to explore play-dough. Here are some ideas to help promote different types of fine-motor skills and to keep the experience interesting:

▶ Give your child a variety of different types of tools to use. These can include such things as rolling pins, plastic knives, scissors, cookie cutters—anything to inspire her to manipulate the play-dough in different ways.

▶ Invite your child to form the dough with her hands into different shapes. Play with your child and model the making of a ball or a snake, using words to help describe what you are doing with your hands so your child will connect words like "rolling the dough" with the action.

▶ Invite your child to mix different objects into the dough or mix the colors. Use these experiences to promote concepts such as bumpy or smooth and to build on your child's ability to recognize colors.

▶ Take play-dough outdoors for more types of discovery such as making leaf prints on the dough or using the dough as a foundation for building with sticks and rocks.

Reflect, Revise, Revisit

Sitting down with your child to explore the process of manipulating and creating with play-dough will make the experience fun for both of you. Use the time to study your child's ability to manipulate the dough in different ways and to identify terms such as rolling, cutting, pinching, and so forth. Exploring play-dough is rich with opportunities to build vocabulary and strengthen fine-motor skills. Additional reading: Play Dough on Pinterest (*www.pinterest.com/teachpreschool/play-dough/*).

CHAPTER 3

Large-Motor Movement Skills

The ability to walk, run, jump, skip, hop, march, kick, stretch, and bend are just a few examples of large-motor skills young children naturally begin to explore as they get ready for kindergarten. Some of these skills take more practice than others to master, but each plays a role in giving young children a sense of competence and confidence as they seek out new challenges or encounter opportunities to join in both organized and unorganized games and activities.

Prior to entering school, your child should be able to demonstrate his skills and knowledge in different types of large-motor skills. As your child's awareness of large-motor movement develops, he should be able to identify the difference between different types of skills, such as bending and stretching, both through actions and through words.

There are both natural and organized ways you can help your child build large-motor skills.

You can spend time playing outdoors or at a local park where there are many natural opportunities to develop large-motor skills. Your child needs both the space and the freedom to run, jump, and climb.

While you are out and about with your child, make up games. Simple ones such as jumping over cracks in the sidewalk or playing "follow the leader" as you march or hop along can lead to more practice in developing large-motor language and skills.

Provide different tools for large-motor play including Hula-Hoops, jump ropes, balls, and riding toys. Any tool for play that encourages new and different kinds of large-motor skills can help your child build competence and confidence.

Large-motor skills can and should be fostered in the indoor environment as well. It is important for your child to know how to control his large-motor movements in a smaller space. Good activities can range from making an obstacle course of furniture to dancing and marching to lively music.

Make indoor games that promote large-motor skills. Make an action cube out of a square box. Print or draw pictures of different action words on each side of the cube and then invite your child to roll the cube to see which action will land on top. When an action lands on top, invite your child to identify and demonstrate the action word or picture.

Indoor and outdoor, large-motor movement opportunities are equally important in helping your child prepare for success in kindergarten. Make sure your child is given ample time outdoors for freedom to move and indoors for refining those movements.

As a parent, you will need to develop the habit of recognizing the kinds of large-motor skills your child most often uses and least often uses. Your child will most likely not be equally proficient in all types of large-motor skills and this is to be expected. As you observe your child, you will be able to identify specific skills that may need more attention. Use your observations to come up with new games to play or as a source of inspiration when you spend the day playing at a park or hiking in the woods.

In this chapter, we'll go over some activities that will help you in your quest to strengthen your child's large-motor skills.

BUILDING BALANCE

Balance is a large-motor skill that can easily be taken for granted, but as your child enters the kindergarten classroom, he will be playing with others in a variety of ways that will require a strong sense of balance.

What Your Child Should Know

Your child should be able to demonstrate:

▶ A working knowledge of the word "balance" and what it means to balance objects as he walks across a room

▶ An understanding of how to keep his body in balance as he moves along a line

How You Can Help

Here are a few simple ideas for helping your child develop the skill to balance and the knowledge of keeping things in balance:

▶ Invite your child to outline a path on the floor, using a single line of painter's tape. (Painter's tape is best for this type of activity and should be removed from the floor after you're done so it doesn't get too tacky and hard to pull up.) Invite your child to try walking on the path, keeping both feet on the line at all times. Model the use of arms to help keep his body in balance. As your child gets more proficient in walking on the line, make the process more challenging by putting things on the line to step over or by walking backward instead of forward.

▶ Look for natural opportunities to build balance either in walking (such as walking across a log) or carrying (for instance, carrying a stack of towels from one room to another). The building of balance requires different kinds of concentration depending on the type of balancing the child is doing.

▶ Play simple balancing games with your child. Stand on one foot and, holding the position, see how high you can count. Now switch to the other foot and count again.

Reflect, Revise, Revisit

Opportunities for building balance arise throughout the day. As you see your child putting away toys such as blocks, for example, does your child show an ability to organize and balance a set of blocks to carry across the room? Does he move the blocks one at a time? Does your child demonstrate an ability to control his body when walking on a path or a balance beam? Can he keep his balance, then freeze and stand in place? Take notice of your child's use of balance and look for fun and natural opportunities to help your child continue these skills over time.

BOUNCY BALLS

Your child will be participating in a variety of games and activities that involve the handling of balls in kindergarten.

What Your Child Should Know

She should demonstrate a basic ability and knowledge of what it means to roll, throw, toss, bounce, and kick a ball.

How You Can Help

Introduce your child to a variety of games and activities that include the use of balls. There are many different kinds of games that require the skilled handling of balls, but for developing the fundamental abilities, here are a few simple games that you can play with your child.

▶ **GIANT STEPS:** Have your child stand about four feet away from you. Roll the ball to her and invite her to roll it back. Now invite her to take one giant step backward and roll the ball again. Every time your child catches the ball when you roll it to her, take another step back. If one of you misses the ball, take a giant step forward. Once your child has the basic idea down, you can change the game to tossing or bouncing the ball back and forth. Continue to take giant steps forward or backward between each toss or bounce of the ball.

▶ **WALK THE DOG:** This ball game gets your child moving as well as practicing ball-handling skills. Choose a starting point and an ending point for your walk, keeping it in a straight line for now. Invite your child to bounce the ball while standing still; then try bouncing the ball while walking from the starting point to the ending point. As her bouncing ability builds, you can add obstacles for her to bounce around.

Ball-handling skills can also develop naturally as your child participates in everyday play like shooting hoops with a basketball, playing catch, or kicking a ball around the yard. Have a variety of types and sizes of balls to play with, and remember it is much more fun to play ball with a partner than all by yourself.

Reflect, Revise, Revisit

Not every child has a natural interest in playing with balls, so you will want to encourage your child's play by making up fun games. For the purpose of building ball-handling skills, make the games about trying new ways to handle a ball rather than on winning or losing a game. Some children will give up on playing games if they're always about winning or losing. Choose games that help your child feel competent and successful in his or her efforts to roll, kick, catch, or bounce the ball!

SPORTSMANSHIP

Being a good sport is a tough concept for kids to wrap their minds around. Young children naturally want to be the first in line or the winner of every game, and when they don't win or get to be first, they can find it frustrating. It is hard for young children to think past their own wants or needs or past their immediate circumstances and consider the possibilities that are ahead. Sportsmanship isn't a skill that is taught in a single lesson—rather it is an ongoing process of building character, empathy, kindness, patience, self-awareness, community awareness, and self-control.

What Your Child Should Know

Sportsmanship has many aspects. Your child should know:

▶ That when things do not go the way he expected them to go it is still important to keep trying

▶ How to express feelings of frustration or disappointment to others in such a way that helps him continue to be a positive member of his community

▶ How to show others that he cares about them

How You Can Help

All of the lessons listed above take time, opportunity, and will most likely be developed after a few tears are shed along the way. As a parent you can help your child by patiently guiding him through the tears and toward a new understanding of each situation. Here are some natural opportunities to help him learn to manage his feelings and develop self-control and patience.

▶ Play simple board games or travel games in which your child may not end up the winner at times. If he gets upset about losing, help him have perspective on what is so upsetting. Ask why he is upset and invite conversation about the situation and the feelings he has about the situation. Remember, expressing feelings or disappointment isn't wrong. What's harmful is to express those feelings in a way that causes harm to your child or to others. Keep the focus on helping your child constructively express his feelings of disappointment or frustration.

▶ Be a role model of good sportsmanship-like behavior for your child.

▶ Give your child plenty of opportunities to play games with other children his own age and the appropriate space he needs to work through frustrating or disappointing moments without your intervention. As young children go through natural childhood conflicts or disappointments in a safe environment, they will begin to develop healthy skills for overcoming these problems later in life.

▶ Be a good listener and send out an open invitation for your child to talk through his feelings of frustration with you. Sometimes the feelings being expressed may not sound reasonable or rational, but his ability to verbalize those frustrations constructively to you or others is part of the process of developing a healthy sense of self-worth and self-control.

▶ If your child happens to be on the winning end of most games, help him be respectful of others rather than being boastful or inconsiderate.

▶ Help your child to reflect on his own behavior and the behavior of others. Where needed, help him talk through what else could have been said or done to make a situation more positive for everyone involved.

The process of building good sportsmanship is an ongoing effort of trial and error, conversations, and experiences that will require your patient guidance and support along the way.

Reflect, Revise, Revisit

Assessing sportsmanship can be both easy and complex, depending on your child's personality. As he is interacting with others you will be able to observe your child's response to winning or losing, getting his way or not getting his way, and being first or being last in line. Use his responses as an opportunity to gauge whether or not healthy habits are being formed and as a basis for providing guidance and support where needed. Engage him in conversations that will lead him in the direction of good decisions and a healthy sense of self-worth and self-control.

PART II

Building Confidence as You Go

Throughout the early childhood years, young children gradually build their sense of self-awareness as well as an awareness of others and the role others play in their lives. It is during these sensitive years that children formulate a belief system about who they are and what they can do. They develop a coping system for balancing or managing emotions such as disappointment, excitement, frustration, and happiness. Finally, it is during these sensitive years that young children begin to exercise their independence while at the same time developing responsibility and respect for others. The preschool years are filled with many social and emotional challenges that can have a lasting impact on a child's ability to do well in school. In this section, you will discover a broad range of ways you can help your child develop a positive belief system and a constructive coping system while at the same time nurturing a sense of responsibility, independence, and confidence.

CHAPTER 4

I Can Be Responsible

When it comes to helping young children develop a sense of personal responsibility there is no better place than home. Yet, it can be at home where young children (or even teenagers) are least likely to demonstrate such a sense.

The obstacles in promoting personal responsibility at home can involve anything from a battle of the wills between parent and child to the "it's not fair" debate between siblings. You'll be forced to wonder just how much patience you have while waiting for little Johnny to pick up the five hundred Legos he dumped all over the floor. Still, these obstacles have to be confronted.

In the kindergarten classroom, your child will be expected to do her fair share of the clean-up in the classroom. The environment naturally promotes personal responsibility through the daily schedule, the classroom set-up, peer pressure, and the teacher's approach to managing a large group of children all at the same time.

However, personal responsibility goes beyond just putting toys away. It's a big word that involves a great deal of complex thinking. It means understanding how the decisions we make, deep down inside, ultimately impact others as well as ourselves; it means taking ownership of those decisions. For the purpose of entering the kindergarten classroom, let's take a look at some basic situations that involve a child's development of personal responsibility.

CLEAN-UP TIME

In the kindergarten classroom, your child will be expected to do her share of taking care of the classroom environment. This can include anything from picking up blocks after play to throwing away trash after snack to putting books back on a shelf and the list goes on.

What Your Child Should Know

Responsibility has many aspects. Your child should:

▶ Know how to organize and put things away in her room and around the home environment

▶ Notice whether a task is fully completed or if there is still some work left to do

▶ Bring to the kindergarten classroom a broad array of skills and abilities to confidently complete the tasks involved in taking care of the classroom environment

How You Can Help

There are many skills that help a young child successfully participate in clean-up such as sorting, folding, wiping, and so on. Let's take a look at a few of those skills and how you can foster each of them at home. By recognizing the skills that help your child to take care of her environment, you will start to understand how each of these skills, when put together, create a competent and capable clean-up time helper.

▶ **SORTING AND CLASSIFYING:** One of the most basic skills in clean-up time is the ability to sort objects and put things that are alike together. For example, if you want your child to put her clothes in a drawer, chances are you want the socks to go in a sock drawer and the pants to go in the pants drawer. Sorting and classifying can teach a child how to organize her world and will be something your child will experience often in the kindergarten classroom. She'll be sorting blocks and toys and crayons and other items as a daily part of helping to put things away. As you seek to help your child get organized, take time to break down the process into specific parts and look for interesting materials and opportunities to sort and classify (like silverware in a drawer) at home.

▶ **FOLDING:** Whether your child is trying to fold a towel or a napkin, folding is a skill that needs time and attention. In the kindergarten classroom your child may be asked to fold dress-up clothes and stack them in a basket or fold a piece of paper to make a snowflake. The practice of folding different kinds of materials varies for each kind of material. Give your child the task of folding a set of towels or folding a sheet of paper to tuck into an envelope. Folding is another way your child can take care of and organize her world.

▶ **STACKING:** In the kindergarten classroom your child will most likely be helping to stack blocks in the block center or neatly stacking a set of books on a shelf. You can give her fun and meaningful opportunities for stacking things at home. Try seeing how high she can stack a set of towels before they fall over. Talk to her about why the towels fell over. Does she need to limit the height of the stack? Also talk to her about the different directions that objects can be stacked. A set of books can be stacked on top of one another or beside one another. Those same books can be stacked from smallest to largest. Look for opportunities to help her explore and practice the skill of stacking.

▶ **CLEARING AND WIPING:** At some point in kindergarten your child will probably be responsible for clearing her place at the table after snack or lunchtime. She'll have to learn how to carry trash to the trash can in one trip and make sure everything else has been neatly removed from the table. At home, you can help your child by encouraging her to set and clear the table before and after a meal. But not all wiping has to be related to housework. Teach her how to wipe a chalkboard clean or give her a squeegee to wipe off the windows of a car (in the summertime, kids will love the opportunity to get wet!). You can find lots of things for your child to wipe, and keeping the process fun will help her develop this skill.

▶ **POURING:** Another skill that your child may need to practice is pouring a drink into her own cup. In some classrooms, children are expected to pour their own juice or water. You can give your child plenty of practice by adding a plastic cup and pitcher to the bathtub or placing a set by the bathroom sink. Encourage your child to fill the cup with water and notice when the cup starts to get too full. Encourage your child to think ahead about how full to get the cup before she starts to fill it up and how to hold the pitcher over the cup rather than resting it on the cup. Remember to use a variety of pitchers because each one pours in a different way. When you feel your child is ready, invite her to pour her own drink at lunch or dinner time. In the end, this process may make for a few spills, but as your child masters the skill of pouring, it will build independence and prevent future messes at the classroom table.

▶ **EVERYTHING HAS ITS PLACE:** In the kindergarten classroom, everything belongs somewhere. Books go on the bookshelf, coats go on hooks, papers go in baskets . . . and the list goes on. Keeping a classroom organized is a must in order to keep children focused and successful in their learning environment. In a child's bedroom, it is easy for him to leave laundry on the floor or crayons on the bedside table, but when these behaviors are left unattended they also develop into bad habits. Get your child into the habit of looking around his room at the end of a day and noticing what items need to be put back in their places. Putting things away doesn't have to be a burdensome chore. It can also be a game. Purposely mix things up a bit—leave a chair upside down or wear a sock on your hand. When your child notices, just say, "Oh, so this isn't where this belongs?" Then invite him to help you make the correction.

▶ **COMPLETING A TASK:** When your child has been given a task, he should learn to notice if the task is complete or if there are parts of it left unfinished. In the kindergarten classroom, your child will be expected to complete a task and not leave the rest for his fellow classmates or teacher. At home, you can help your child notice if a task has been completed. Start with simple jobs such as putting away a basket of toys. Are all the toys in the basket or are there still some under the bed or behind the basket? Teach your child to take a look around to make sure that the work is fully completed before moving on to something else.

What you don't want to do is create anxiety over cleaning up. Instead, break the routine into smaller tasks that your child can successfully complete. Even in the kindergarten classroom, the teacher will not send your child into a messy classroom and simply say, "I need you to clean all of this up before I get back." Instead, the teacher will expect your child to complete specific tasks that help the classroom as a whole.

Reflect, Revise, Revisit

Remember that clean-up time is a set of skills, not just one skill. Those skills can be taught both through playful activities and through working on household chores. The goal is to help your child be successful in completing tasks and to take pride in his efforts. As your child is completing a task, reflect on what seems to be missing from his collection of skills and think of games or fun ways to give that skill a little more attention. Don't always associate every process of learning a skill with clean-up time, but do use clean-up time as a way to assess the skills your child may still need more experience to master.

RESPECT

Personal responsibility also involves the concept of respect—respect for others, respect for things, and self-respect.

What Your Child Should Know

Your child should know:

▶ That it is important to demonstrate respect for others and the property of others

▶ How her actions demonstrate a sense of respect

How You Can Help

As your child heads off into the kindergarten classroom, respect will be an important part of her success in the classroom and an important ongoing learning process. Some children naturally develop a sense of respect early on while others need more guidance in this area. Here are a few tips for helping your child develop a sense of respect.

▶ To help your child understand the effect respect has on others, use the term "respect" when showing appreciation for something your child has done or said that makes you happy or proud. For example, you might say, "Picking this flower for your teacher is so thoughtful. What a respectful and kind gesture." In other words, combine the word "respect" with other words (such as kindness) that give the word a positive meaning.

▶ To help your child build a healthy respect for herself and for other people, model the concept of respect. Let your child catch you showing respect to others through your actions or words. Purposely let your child hear you say something respectful about her teacher or others in her life. Let your child overhear you say something respectful and loving about her to a friend or another parent.

▶ Play simple games that teach the actual word and concept of respect in a more hands-on way. For example, pick out two baskets. Make one of the baskets bright and pretty (this will be your respect basket) and make the other basket old and dingy (this will be your disrespect basket). Fill your disrespect basket with items you have collected around the house that are lacking in respect: torn books, a broken toy, a stuffed animal with a missing button, or a dirty cup. Tell your child that the items in your "disrespect basket" want to be moved to the "respect basket" and only she can help them out. Invite her to figure out with you why the object landed in the disrespect basket in the first place and then what can be done to help the item move over to the happy and very pretty respect basket!

Finally, remember that role-play is an excellent tool for acting out the way your child interacts with the people in her life. Take time to do a little role-playing with her. You can be the grouchy kid and she can be the kind parent. See where she goes with the role-play and have fun being "disrespectful" but always end your play with the message that being respectful makes everyone feel much better.

Reflect, Revise, Revisit

Be observant of your child's words and actions. If you see that she is struggling to show respect for others or for things belonging to others, look for the reasons why. Perhaps your child was just tired or was feeling angry. Help her look for ways to express her feelings and needs without being disrespectful to others. You may need to help your child learn to verbalize her frustration or you may need to make sure she gets more sleep. There will be times when others may not deserve your child's respect, but the message for her must remain constant. The concept of respect can be so complex and it will probably take time and certainly a consistent message in order for your child to sort it all out. With your patient guidance and example, your child will get the message you are trying to share.

COOPERATION

In the kindergarten classroom, your child will work and play in cooperation with other children. Participating in this sort of activity is another aspect of taking personal responsibility. For a young child, this can be a challenging task because it requires him to set aside some of his own wants and needs to accommodate those of others.

What Your Child Should Know

Your child should know or have a good understanding of what it means to work or play cooperatively with others.

How You Can Help

Just as we said concerning respect, cooperation is the kind of skill that you can model and influence. However, cooperation can also be demonstrated through many fun and hands-on games and activities. Since cooperation is all about working together, these games require at least two people. Here is one example of a cooperation game you can play with your child:

▶ **PARACHUTE PALS:** The objective of this game is to help your child understand the value of cooperating. The lesson is that if one person doesn't cooperate, the game really won't be much fun. However, if both pals cooperate and do their part, the game will be great.

To set up the parachute-pals game, place three or four balls on a lightweight piece of fabric or perhaps even a small tablecloth. Have your child grab one end of the fabric while you grab the other end.

While both pals are holding on to the fabric, give it a brisk shake to see how high you can toss the balls and catch them when they come down. What happens when one person lets go of his end of the fabric? Will the balls continue to soar high into the air? What if one person refuses to hold his end of the fabric—would the game be any fun? As you play parachute pals with your child, purposely let go of your end of the fabric and then say, "Hey! We need some cooperation here!" Your child will probably want to let go of his end of the fabric too, and each time you can repeat the phrase, "Hey! We need some cooperation here!"

Reflect, Revise, Revisit

By making up fun games that require cooperation and using the term "cooperation" during the games, your child should quickly become familiar with what the word means. Invite him to help you make up other games that require two people. You can brainstorm a few ideas together. As your child demonstrates the understanding that it takes at least two people to play the game, he is well on the way to understanding what it means to play cooperatively with others.

KINDNESS

In most kindergarten classrooms, kindness will be a standard part of the curriculum and a feature of the rules of the classroom. Kindness is also a part of developing a sense of personal responsibility for your choices in how you treat others. It is important that young children understand how to be kind to others so that all children can feel safe and accepted in the classroom environment.

What Your Child Should Know

Your child should know how to intentionally show kindness towards others and be able to recognize kind actions.

How You Can Help

Again, as we talked about in the section on respect, you can model kindness every day at home. As your child reaps the benefit of your kindness and sees how you behave toward others, he will learn the value of kindness as well as how to be kind himself. As a fun way to encourage your child to show acts of kindness towards others, you can invite your child to start a "kindness project."

▶ To set up the kindness project, invite your child to help you cut a nice supply of different colors of hearts out of construction paper (this is also a good time for your child to practice his cutting skills!). Place all the hearts in an envelope with the label "Kindness Project" on the outside of the envelope.

Invite your child to share one of his kindness hearts with others whenever he sees a person being kind to others or when he just wants to show kindness to others. Your child will discover that noticing acts of kindness and sharing acts of kindness (giving a heart away) makes others happy—and that will make your child happy, too.

You can extend this process by creating your own kindness board. Each time you see your child or anyone one else in your family doing something unexpected and kind for others, place a heart on the board and write on the heart what act of kindness you observed. Invite the whole family to join in your child's kindness project and look for acts of kindness to fill up your board.

Reflect, Revise, Revisit

When you and your child are in social situations, take time to notice how your child responds and speaks to others. Does he make an effort to show kindness? In what ways do you see him demonstrating his kindness to others? To reinforce the message of kindness, give your child a little positive feedback for his efforts by talking about the act of kindness you observed.

As your child's kindness project is underway, take a few minutes to invite him tell you about the acts of kindness he observed. As your child describes the acts of kindness to you, you will be able to assess his understanding and perspective about what it means to be kind and how to show kindness to others.

CHAPTER 5

I'll Be Okay!

For some children, and parents, the prospect of heading off to kindergarten can cause some first-day jitters. This is normal for even the most prepared child, so let's discuss it.

FIRST-DAY JITTERS

The ideas and activities in this book are designed to help your child feel prepared for kindergarten. As your child develops a sense of self-confidence and independence, and masters the skills identified throughout this book, you both should be more than ready to embrace the kindergarten experience. However, no matter how prepared your child may be, it would not be that unusual for her to feel some jitters about going to the first day of kindergarten.

What Your Child Should Know

Your child should know:

- That she is going to be a great kindergarten student

- What she should expect while at kindergarten

- Who will be there to care for and teach her during the day

- That you will be waiting for her at the end of her fun day and will be excited to see and hear all about her amazing day in kindergarten

How You Can Help

Here are a few tips to help your child get a good start on her first day of kindergarten:

- Invite her to help you set out all the things she will need for this first day of school.

- Let her help you pick out what she wants to wear. It is really better to choose something comfortable to wear than her Sunday best, so you may want to separate school clothing from nonschool clothing to narrow down the clothing choices and hopefully avoid any potential decision-making stress.

- Make sure your child gets a good night of sleep before the first day of school. A tired child will be much more emotional and stressed than a well-rested child.

▶ Make sure she is up early and has plenty of time to get ready, so she can relax a bit before heading off to school. Being rushed in the morning can make your child feel more stressed.

▶ Make sure she has a healthy breakfast. Your child will need the extra energy a healthy breakfast can provide.

▶ If you feel it is needed—and if it is possible—take your child to visit her classroom before school begins to meet the teacher. You may need to contact the school in advance to see if this is something it can accommodate.

Reflect, Revise, Revisit

Before the first day of school, you may sense some excitement or jitters about getting ready. Be on the lookout for signs of nervousness such as being overly sensitive or excited. Try to keep your child's day as normal as possible. Over-building his expectations can unintentionally create more jitters, but ignoring the first day can create more stomach butterflies. Relax with your child, run your normal errands, and be open to talking with your child about anything he wants to chat about.

If you are having your own attack of the jitters—and what parent doesn't?—try to keep them in check as well. Your child will sense your mood or anxiousness and can start to worry. Take a deep breath and look for the many positive experiences your child has in store for his future.

SEPARATION ANXIETY

Up to this point in her life, your child has pretty much been exclusively in your company. That is to say, except for visits to relatives, she's always been around you and she knows you're there to take care of any problems. That's about to change, and it's only natural that it should be accompanied by anxiety—for both of you.

What Your Child Should Know

Your child should:

▶ Feel free to express her nervousness, sadness, concern, fear, or even if she is getting a tummy ache whenever she is away from mom or dad

▶ Know that her feelings are valid and that it is okay to share her feelings with you as well as her teacher

▶ Develop strategies, with your help, of how to make the best out of spending time away from you

▶ Plan to come home and tell you all about her time away so her accomplishments can be celebrated together

How You Can Help

If your child has a history of severe separation anxiety, here are some things you might consider trying:

▶ Take your child to visit her kindergarten classroom well before the first day.

▶ Schedule a time to meet with your child's teacher and to share your concerns (without your child present).

▶ Schedule a time for your child to meet her teacher. Ask the teacher if you can take a photo of your child and the teacher doing something simple together.

▶ Keep the teacher's photo displayed on the refrigerator and casually bring up the teacher's name in conversation. The idea is to make the teacher feel like a familiar person in your child's world.

▶ Long before school begins, help your child adjust to separating from you by going to a friend's house to play while you run a few errands or by going to a Sunday School class while you are attending adult services. Look for opportunities to give your child brief experiences in time away from you.

▶ If your child seems ready, consider enrolling her in a mommy's day out program or a part-time preschool class. This will give her even more time and experience being without her mom or dad.

Reflect, Revise, Revisit

If your efforts don't seem to be helping your child adjust more easily to spending time away from you, consider talking with her teacher or school guidance counselor for further support.

Seek out additional resources on the topic of separation anxiety so you can learn other methods and tips for helping your child have a successful school experience. For additional information on separation anxiety see: Separation Anxiety: How to Handle First Day Fears (*www.education .com/magazine/article/How_Handle_Separation_Anxiety*) and Separation Anxiety Discussion and Resource (*www.teach preschool.org/2010/08/separation-anxiety-give-away*). Continue to read and apply the tips and ideas shared throughout this book. As you seek to foster your child's readiness, your child will begin to build the skills she needs to leave your side and confidently enter the kindergarten classroom.

A POSITIVE SELF-IMAGE

Every child needs to start his kindergarten experience with a healthy sense of self-worth and a strong belief in his abilities to succeed. A positive self-image leads to greater confidence and a happier experience. A negative self-image can hold a child back from wanting to try new things or can make him worry too much about "getting everything right" when the goal should be to "give your best effort."

What Your Child Should Know

Your child should know that the most important job he has right now is to give every task or every challenge his very best effort.

How You Can Help

Focus your praise on the effort your child puts into something rather than on the outcome. Let's examine this principle a little more closely:

▶ Let's say that your child painted a picture of a flower. The flower is the outcome of the painting process. When he shows you the flower, look past the outcome and at the process instead.

▶ When looking at the process, you discover that the real beauty of this painting is the effort your child put into it. His artistry may have included skills like selecting specific colors to paint with, taking more time to paint than usual, or deftly using the paintbrush to make long swishing strokes.

▶ Look for opportunities to genuinely praise your child on the efforts made. Whether your child is painting, solving a puzzle, or choosing which socks to wear, you want your child to be excited about trying again—for with repeated attempts, he'll master new skills.

Reflect, Revise, Revisit

Keeping in mind that your child's positive self-image comes from the belief and confidence that he is capable of accomplishing simple to complex goals or tasks, take notice of how often he tackles or completes a task without asking for your assistance. If your child is constantly saying "I can't" or "I don't know how" or "Will you do it for me?" continue to encourage him to give it his best effort and then look for opportunities to celebrate that effort together.

CHAPTER 6

It's All about Me

As children begin that journey that leads them away from the home environment, they will want to bring with them information that keeps them connected to home and have the ability to tell others, when needed or desired, "This is who I am!"

I KNOW MY NAME

To a child, her name is very special and meaningful. A child's name gives her a sense of identity and self-worth.

What Your Child Should Know

Before heading off to kindergarten, your child should:

▶ Be familiar with her full name

▶ Be able to recite to others, when asked or when needed, what her first and last names are

You'll find further discussion on name recognition and writing later in this book.

How You Can Help

There are lots of fun ways to reinforce your child's name over time.

► Make up a name song. For example, change the words to a familiar tune like "London Bridge" to say, "There's a boy who has two names, has two names, has two names. There's a boy who has two names. I wonder what they are?" See if your child can answer the question.

► Play a Name Game. For example, show your child how to tap her hands on knees and then clap hands together. Now create a tapping to clapping pattern with the two hand motions. While clapping and tapping the pattern with your hands start a rhythmical chant like this: "My first name is _____." "My last name is _____." "Now can you tell me your name?" Take turns going back and forth filling in the blank with your own name, your child's name, and the name of any other person who might be joining in the fun.

Reflect, Revise, Revisit

Through casual conversation and other opportunities, verbalize your child's full name so that she can hear it being spoken by you. In addition, and where you feel it is appropriate in your circumstances, give your child some background on her full name:

▶ How is your child's name different or the same as yours?

▶ Does your child's name have a special meaning?

▶ Was your child named after someone else in the family?

If she still has trouble remembering her full name, you might select a designated parent, grandparent, or other member to start addressing your child by her full name on a regular basis to help her connect with the name a little more easily.

I KNOW MY AGE AND BIRTHDAY

Age is a big deal for prekindergarten- and kindergarten-age kids, so help your child have a good grasp on when he will be turning to the next big number!

What Your Child Should Know

Your child should:

▶ Know how old he is

▶ Have a good grasp of the date of his birthday

How You Can Help

Find or make a nice-sized calendar to display the months and days of the year so your child can keep track of special occasions, like a birthday, that will soon be coming. A calendar is a good way to help your child begin to understand the concept of yesterday, today, and tomorrow and to begin understanding basic math concepts as he counts how many more days it will be until his birthday or until the first day of school.

▶ You can make a simple calendar by drawing the basic grid for a calendar on a large poster board. Have a set of blank cards or sticky notes on which your child can help print numbers and pictures to add to the calendar each day. Display your child's calendar where he can see it, and keep the process fun and accessible.

▶ Invite your child to help you decorate a few extra blank calendar cards or sticky notes to represent special events. For example, your child could draw a birthday cake to represent his birthday or a big number 5 to represent how old he will be. Invite him to draw a symbol that will best help him remember what that special day is all about.

▶ Help your child place the special event cards on the correct month and day of the calendar. Invite your child to print the number and add the next number each day throughout the calendar month. It is okay if he gets off track a bit during the month; the goal is to show a progression of time and not to ensure accuracy in calendar making.

▶ Use your child's calendar as an opportunity to talk about how many days until his birthday and what day of the month his birthday falls.

▶ You can use the calendar to invite new understanding of other concepts like number recognition, counting, time, seasons, weather, and more.

Reflect, Revise, Revisit

Ask your child to help you keep track of a variety of activities such as what day you went to the grocery store or how many more days until you get to go to the movies. Choose short goals that will happen within a few days or weeks so that your child will not lose interest in the countdown. The more you integrate the calendar into your daily life, the more your child will begin to take notice of the different components of a calendar as well as gain a sense of time (yesterday, today, tomorrow). He'll come to understand how time comes and goes and how the calendar helps us track the days and events in our lives. Use the opportunity to ask your child to remind you when his birthday falls. Explore the calendar with your child—don't just be a provider of facts. Your child will find calendar time a fun way to explore time, seasons, events, experiences, and plans along with you.

I KNOW THE MEMBERS OF MY FAMILY

The members of a child's family are the most important people in her life. As she prepares to head off to kindergarten, she'll want to tell her teacher or friends about her mom or dad or tell stories about places her family goes together and things they do. The more knowledge your child has about her family, the more easily she will be able to talk about them.

What Your Child Should Know

Your child should know:

▶ That Mommy's name is not just "Mommy"

▶ That Mommy and all the other members of the family have real names, too

▶ A few simple facts about your family and extended family

How You Can Help

Create a family journal that your child can keep and write or draw in.

▶ Provide family photos for your child to add to her journal. As your child selects and adds new photos to the journal, point out the members of the family that are in each photo and the names they use.

▶ The photos you give your child can be photocopies or printouts for your child to cut out and glue in her journal.

▶ Offer to help your child print the names of each family member in the journal. As your child is ready, she can attempt to write the names on her own.

▶ As you are adding photos to your child's family journal, talk about what is happening in each photo or the memories you have of each photo. Tell family stories that give meaning and history behind the photos.

▶ Consider adding childhood photos of you, your parents, and your grandparents (and those of your spouse, of course) for additional discussion on the history of your family, what you were like as a child, and what name your friends or parents called you. This will help your child develop perspective on who her family is or was.

Reflect, Revise, Revisit

As your child's photo journal begins to have a nice selection of photos to flip through, invite him to show his journal to you (or to others) and share with you which photos he enjoys looking at the most. Take the opportunity to ask him if he can remember the stories you told about the photos and what names are printed below or beside each photo. Invite your child to tell you his own stories about the photos. You might be surprised at the stories you will hear, but just go with it and enjoy his interest in telling you a story. While taking a walk through your child's journal, remember to draw connections between the printed names or words that were added to the journal and the photos they represent.

I KNOW WHERE I LIVE

As you prepare your child for kindergarten, now is a good time to introduce her to her home address and the surrounding community. Knowing a home address and recognizing the surrounding community will be helpful in situations when your child is away from home. For example, she should be able to recognize familiar landmarks on the path between school and home. She should be able to tell a teacher or bus driver "I live in the Westview Apartments."

WHAT YOUR CHILD SHOULD KNOW

There are several parts to a child's understanding of where he or she lives. Your child should have a good grasp on:

► The ability to describe her home to others

► Her home address or the most significant parts of it

► Where her home is located in relation to a local school, park, or other places she goes often and finds important in her daily life

How You Can Help

Trying to remember a complete home address might be more than your child is ready for, but focusing on specific parts of your address can help her communicate those essential parts to a trusted adult—should there be a need.

Helping a child learn to recite her address can be nothing more than a process of memorizing certain facts, but you can help to put some of those facts into perspective by helping your child draw connections between the facts and real-life things.

▶ If your home address is on the mailbox or on the house, show your child where the numbers are and explain how these numbers are a part of identifying your home address. Perhaps even take your child next door to see how the numbers change and continue to get larger or smaller as you go down the street.

▶ Take your child on a little drive or walk down your street and find the sign that identifies the name of your street. Invite your child to help you count how many other houses are on the same street or to find other buildings, signs, or landmarks that line up along the street you live.

▶ Follow the clues. Exploring mail can be a mystery game because each word or number on a letter is a clue to where it's going and where it is coming from. Mail your child a letter to your home address (or ask someone else to mail your child a letter—kids love mail!). When the letter arrives, give your child the unopened mail, a set of crayons or markers, some paper, and a new envelope.

Invite him to look for clues on the unopened envelope that might identify whom the mail is for, what address it was sent to, where the stamp is, where the mail came from, and so forth. Ask him to use the markers to circle the different parts of the address found on the envelope.

▶ After your child has looked for the clues, it is time to open the mail and see what is inside! Then write a letter back. If your child's "address" on the envelope doesn't look quite right for mailing, no worries—just tuck it into a second envelope with all the right information and send it. The goal is to invite your child to explore the process, not to get it perfectly right.

Prekindergarten-age children are often fascinated by making and following a map. A map also provides clues to a mystery, and mapmaking can be a fun and intriguing way to get your child drawing, writing, and putting his perspective down on paper.

▶ Take a drive or walk around your neighborhood. Invite your child to notice landmarks between your home and his school. Are there any special buildings, signs, trees, or other landmarks that are interesting and meaningful to your child along the way? How many streets or turns must you travel to get there from your home?

▶ Following your excursion, make a simple map on a large sheet of paper. Invite your child to draw the roads and landmarks that you and he discovered. Assist him where needed and add names of other buildings or streets if you like.

▶ The goal of mapmaking is not to create an accurate map but to explore the landmarks and to give your child an idea of where his home is in respect to his school or other familiar places. It will help him notice his surroundings and to begin recognizing familiar landmarks in his community.

▶ Your child may wish to take his map on your next trip to follow along and see if there are other landmarks he might have missed. That's great! Continue mapmaking as your child continues to show interest.

Reflect, Revise, Revisit

As your child participates in mapmaking or receiving and writing mail, he'll be gaining a sense of where his home is located in the community and that his home has an address uniquely its own. You can find out the extent of your child's knowledge through casual conversation while you are checking the mail or driving down the road.

For instance, you can play a travel game. Ask your child to tell you what he thinks will be coming up around the next corner or how many more houses until you get to your own.

You can also ask your child to help sort the mail by name or numbers or type of mail. If he helps often, it won't take long before he will start to recognize familiar names and numbers but, on occasion, you are going to want to make sure there is some mail mixed in the batch for him, too!

▶ Look for a variety of other mail-sorting possibilities. Invite your child to help you decorate a few shoeboxes for sorting mail. Let your child take the lead in how he wants to sort the mail. He may wish to sort the mail by type, color, or shape. While sorting mail, continue to draw attention to your home address and to reinforce name recognition. Young children remember facts best when they are given opportunities to explore the information through hands-on, real-life experiences.

I KNOW MY PHONE NUMBER AND HOW TO SAY "HELLO!"

In today's world of cellular phone technology, there is ample opportunity and access for young children to learn to operate a phone by doing more than making phone calls. Your child may already have extensive experience in playing games or watching a video on your cell phone. In fact, many homes no longer even have what could be referred to as "an old-fashioned home telephone" or land line. In addition, most adults enter friends and family in the contact section of their cell phones, so when needing to make a phone call it is no longer necessary to look at the actual telephone number.

What Your Child Should Know

With the advances in technology, it is even more important to make sure your child has a sense of how to reach you by phone. After all, not every telephone your child may need to use will have that contact name already plugged in. With that in mind, your child should know:

▶ How to use all kinds of telephones and what series of numbers will need to be pressed into the phone before pushing the send button

▶ How to hold a meaningful conversation over the telephone

▶ How to listen to what is being said by the voice at the other end of the line and then respond

All of this takes some practice. Communication via current technology is more prevalent in your child's world than ever before, and it is important not to take their understanding of today's communication technology for granted.

How You Can Help

Begin with the basics. Help your child know that every phone has its own phone number.

▶ If you have a recent telephone bill on hand, pull it out and ask your child to circle some of the numbers on the bill. You can say, "This phone number is for Grandma's phone, and this phone number is for the pizza place." If you don't have a bill that shows frequently called numbers, use a phone book or create a list of phone numbers to give your child a visual of how phone numbers belong to a specific person or phone.

▶ Help your child make her own personal contact list. Give her a blank sheet of paper on a clipboard to help her print the names of favorite names of people along with their phone numbers. You can assist her in writing out the most important phone numbers—first your own or a grandparent's phone number. Invite your child to help you think of other phone numbers she would like to add to the contact list.

▶ As your child's contact list grows, you can possibly provide small photos of each person to glue beside the list (much like you can do in a real cell phone contact list). This will help identify which phone number belongs to which person on the list.

▶ Your child may also wish to explore writing out different strings of numbers as a pretend contact list. This is great writing practice and you should give her ample freedom to explore. Invite her to draw a picture of the person beside her phone number. The process of developing a contact list should be open-ended and interesting to your child. Remember to keep a clipboard handy for those lists because there is something interesting and fun to a young child about putting her "work" on a clipboard.

▶ As your child is writing out phone numbers, take the time to reinforce your own phone number. One way to do this is to create a simple phone-number song. Putting the phone number to a familiar tune will help your child draw upon the musical pattern of the numbers and remember that the numbers belong in a specific order.

▶ Ten-Digit Telephone-Number Song

(Tune: "If You're Happy and You Know It!")

If you want to call me up,

(Ring-a-ling)

If you want to call me up,

(Ring-a-ling)

Just dial

555-555-5555

(Ring-a-ling)

▶ After introducing your child to her contact list of phone numbers and the phone-number song, give her some real practice on making a few phone calls. Talk with your child about your set of rules for making calls. Those may include whom your child can call, what times she can call, and so forth.

▶ Build a sense of responsibility toward the person your child is calling. For instance, you might say something like, "If you dial Grandma's phone number, she will be so excited to know you are calling her but very disappointed if all you do is hang up the phone." Your child needs to understand that behind each phone number is a real person with feelings to consider.

▶ Give your child opportunities to talk with you on the phone or with other trusted adults. Demonstrate phone manners such as how to say hello, how to stop and listen, how to respond, and how to say goodbye.

Reflect, Revise, Revisit

Invite your child to sing the phone-number song with you or to help you make a phone call to a trusted friend or family member. As she uses the phone to make real phone calls, you will be able to tell how well she understands making a phone call and what phone numbers she's starting to remember.

Communicating by phone is a special type of skill that takes experience and practice, so don't be in a hurry for your child to develop strong phone manners. But do give your child plenty of opportunities to build her skills. The best way to reflect on your child's progress in communicating by phone is to give her a call—after all, every child loves getting a phone call!

I KNOW MY ALLERGIES

Your child may have food allergies or allergies to dust, insects, or perhaps some household products. Some of these might be easily managed with a dose of Benadryl or by a quick hand washing. However, some allergies may be more severe and result in major health problems or risks. As your child enters a kindergarten classroom, his teacher will need to know what kinds of allergies he has, what kinds of reactions to expect, and how to help manage, address, or prevent allergic reactions. However, you can help your child and his teacher remain aware of allergies that rank high up on your list of priorities by building your child's knowledge of his own allergies and what types of things to avoid handling or eating.

What Your Child Should Know

Although the school should have a list of student allergies on file, your child should:

▶ Have a good working knowledge of any severe allergies that he has.

▶ Know what the symptoms are when he is having an allergic reaction.

▶ Be able to tell a teacher or a friend, "I can't have peanut butter (or fill in the blank) because I am allergic."

Most teachers are now informed of many common food allergies but friends and family may not be. In any case, it is a good idea if your child can specifically inform others of his own allergies that can result in major health risks.

How You Can Help

There are so many kinds of minor allergies that if you focus too much on this problem, you can inadvertently cause your child to become overly concerned. If he feels overanxious about every minor allergen, then he may wind up missing out on many important and interesting experiences. Teach your child how to manage minor allergies. For example, if he can handle a pet only if he washes his hands immediately afterward, teach your child this process for managing a pet allergy. You want your child to be a good manager of his allergies rather than let the allergies take control of his play and other experiences.

▶ For severe allergies (those that cause major health risks), teach your child that it is okay to be assertive in reminding others. Talk with your child about what food items he absolutely cannot eat and how it makes him feel when he does eat them. Help your child to verbalize how he is feeling when having an allergic reaction. However, balance any learning opportunity with helping your child feel better.

Remember that when it comes to any type of allergy, it may take some investigative work on your part to figure out what's going on if the allergic reaction (such as rashes or bumps) persists. Your role is to advocate calmly but consistently for your child as necessary. Remember that when you do this, your child will notice how you handle the situation. If your approach is too aggressive, that in itself can cause your child to become anxious and fearful. Stay calm and teach your child that there is always a way to seek answers and to solve a problem when you approach it in a calm and constructive manner.

Reflect, Revise, Revisit

If you are in the habit of making all the decisions regarding what your child will eat or play with, it is time to include your child more in the decision-making process. As he is more involved, you will naturally be better able to assess your child's understanding of his allergy issues.

▶ Invite your child to cook or bake with you. As he helps you, assist him to identify which parts of the recipe he may need to find a good substitute for and which parts he can safely use. Cooking with your child is a great adventure in building math, science, and daily-living skills, and it can be a fun and natural way to help you judge your child's understanding of the different types of foods he should or should not eat.

▶ Build your child's confidence in telling other adults when he has an allergy that they need to know about. Don't do all the talking for your child; instead, sit back and listen to him tell his allergy stories or experiences to others. As you listen to your child communicate with other people about his allergies, you will be helping him speak up as well as helping yourself understand the degree to which he knows what allergies he has and how to manage them.

▶ Finally, invite your child to apply a little self-care or prevention when it comes to minor allergens. Show him how to wash his hands after touching a pine cone or how to content himself with looking at the bunny rather than petting it. After all, even if petting the bunny feels great, it's not going to be much fun if your child feels miserable afterward. Over time, you can observe and assess your child's ability to make good decisions when it comes to preventing or addressing a minor allergic reaction.

CHAPTER 7

A Community of Learners

As your child enters the kindergarten classroom, she will become a part of a community of learners. To help your child be a successful member of her new kindergarten group, let's take a look at a few of the basic skills that your child will need to be strengthening and developing during the time leading up to and even long after she enters the kindergarten classroom.

Social skills are complex and take time and experiences to develop. They develop best when a child spends time at play with other children her own age. Let's take a look at some of the different aspects of building a solid foundation of social skills.

SPENDING TIME WITH FRIENDS

Friendship is an important part of kindergarten success. Young children need to feel accepted by their peers and have the skills to play cooperatively, productively, and positively with others.

What Your Child Should Know

Entering a new community of peers can be challenging. Your child should know:

▶ How to make new friends in his kindergarten classroom

▶ How to play successfully with others

▶ How to be a good friend to others

How You Can Help

One of the most important things you can do to promote social development in your child is to give him ample time to play with other children his own age. Self-directed play with peers offers young children the opportunity to make up their own rules, negotiate, collaborate, and make decisions. As you seek to provide opportunities for your child to spend time with friends, look for opportunities that will offer ample time in self-directed play. Some options to consider include the following:

▶ Inviting one of your child's friends over to play at your house is one way to give your child quality time and a chance for social interaction. However, try to balance that with a play date at the friend's house as well. Your child needs to experience time with friends both at home and away from home. Location makes a difference in how young children choose to play and the types of skills they develop.

▶ Consider signing your child up for local classes at a gym but remember that in a structured environment, like a gymnastic class, the play is being guided by an instructor rather than being self-directed by your child and his friends. Your child needs a balance of structured and unstructured play-time opportunities.

▶ Think about enrolling your child in a preschool program. Whether he attends a part- or full-time preschool, your child will get the benefit of spending time with a broader range of children than those his own age. However, you should still inquire about the preschool's position on play. If the majority of the day is consumed with instruction and teacher-directed table activities, your child will once again be missing out on the opportunity for self-directed play.

▶ If your child will be attending a half- or full-day prekindergarten class, inquire about the amount of time set aside for self-directed play. If the time is limited, then make your own plans for helping your child get the time he needs in self-directed play.

Reflect, Revise, Revisit

As you reflect on your child's play experiences, consider how much time your child is given to freely play with his friends. Don't monopolize your child's play time with specific plans made by an adult. Any time with friends is valuable to a child, but developing social skills during unstructured, self-directed playtime with a friend is precious.

I'M TALKING TO YOU

Developing the ability to communicate clearly and constructively is another important part of social development and kindergarten success. The ability to express her wants and needs verbally, to tell a story, to share ideas, to ask questions will all be a part of your child's daily interactions with friends and her teacher.

What Your Child Should Know

Your child should know how to communicate confidently and constructively her needs, thoughts, feelings, preferences, choices, and ideas throughout the daily interactions with peers and teachers.

How You Can Help

Communication skills involve a broad range of development, experience, and knowledge. One of many strategies for helping your child develop, practice, and master her ability to communicate effectively is to spend time in conversation with her along with quality time set aside for play and interaction with peers. You can help your child foster her communication skills through a variety of everyday experiences:

▶ Give your child time to play with friends. This will help her learn how to express her views, share ideas, and resolve conflict. Young children naturally engage in some type of role-play; they must negotiate who will be the parent and who will be the child; they must define the rules of the games they are playing—who will go first and who will go last; and they must find ways to get along with each other. As your child plays, she will naturally experience conflict along the way, but as she tries to formulate her thoughts and words in the process of verbally working through the conflict, without parent intervention but within safe boundaries, she is building important communication skills.

▶ Spending time reading together is another effective strategy towards building your child's ability to communicate effectively. As you are reading to your child, you can ask her questions about the book, which will invite conversation and discussion about the characters, illustration, and the story.

▶ Sitting down at the dinner table as a family to eat or play a game is another way to engage your child in conversation. Communication skills are always encouraged as children engage in everyday interactions and conversations with the people they care about the most.

Reflect, Revise, Revisit

Communicating with others effectively and positively takes practice in real-life situations. As your child is playing with friends, take the time to observe the play without interrupting it. Watch your child's interactions and listen to conversations. Take note of how she resolves conflict and only intervene if it is absolutely needed. Give your child time to sort out her play and notice where you might take time later to help give her the "words to say" or suggest choices she could make in future situations. As you guide your child through the thought processes of how to resolve conflict or how to communicate her thoughts, she will develop the skills needed for successful and healthy negotiation, conflict resolution, and interaction—all valuable skills in kindergarten.

Another way to judge how your child is performing with social interaction is in the act of reading. After reading a favorite book several times, invite your child to "read" the book to you. Any words she uses to communicate the story from her own perspective will be great practice in developing the ability to communicate her own ideas and understandings. Remember—this isn't a test in listening skills. This is an invitation to build your child's confidence in communication. Listen to your child's retelling of the story and use the opportunity to reflect on how she communicates the story back to you. Was she able to formulate and verbalize her thoughts clearly? Was she able to recall the main points of the story? Did she feel confident in sharing her thoughts and ideas? Part of developing good communication skills is the ability to feel confident sharing your own ideas and perspectives.

While eating dinner together, ask your child to share something about her day. This will help you understand her ability to formulate thoughts or memories and "tell a story" about the day. Chances are, once she enters kindergarten you will be on the edge of your seat wanting to hear all about how the day went. Begin now by helping your child to formulate and communicate her thoughts. If your child is having trouble verbalizing the events of her day, give a few prompts or ask simple questions to invite her to talk freely.

While playing games with your child, use this time to assess how well she verbalizes or expresses her choices and decisions. If she finds the game frustrating, help her know what words she can use to express her feelings. Try to keep the experience casual and fun rather than a formal test of communication skills. Encourage conversation, laughter, jokes, and silliness. Effective communication involves the ability to communicate easily and constructively all kinds of feelings and emotions.

USE YOUR WALKING FEET

There is every real possibility that your child's kindergarten classroom will have a set of rules posted on the wall. In every community there must be rules, which provide some sense of order and boundaries. The learning community is like a small society, and the teacher provides a sense of order and consistent boundaries. One way a teacher will often help students to understand their role in the learning community is by establishing a set of classroom rules.

What Your Child Should Know

Your child should:

▶ Know what it means to "follow the rules"

▶ Be able to demonstrate a good sense of what it means to follow a set of rules

▶ Understand why it is important to follow the rules

▶ Have the ability to apply and follow the rules to himself and others

How You Can Help

Following rules goes beyond kindergarten. Understanding the idea of rules helps your child play games, follow the rules of the household, or even follow the rules of places you go. Your child should know that rules are designed to keep people safe and to help them understand what is expected of them so everyone can have a happy experience. Here are some things you can do to enhance that learning:

▶ Help your child identify rules throughout his community—for example, at a swimming pool or in a theater. Look for posted signs of rules and draw your child's attention to what they say and invite discussion about the rules you find. What do the rules mean? Who are the rules for? Why do the people in charge have these rules? What might happen if you break a rule? Try to help your child understand that there are consequences to breaking a rule and how following rules can be a good thing.

▶ Suggest to your child that he make up his own set of rules for around the house or for his room. Help him make a sign with three simple rules. Let your child choose what rules he would like to put on the sign. As your child tells you what the rules are, ask him the same questions mentioned in the previous point. Help your child thoughtfully consider all the different types of decisions and consequences that go along with making each rule.

▶ As you are helping your child make and discover rules, talk to him about what kinds of rules there might be at school. Ask thoughtful questions that help your child think about how he will need to be considerate of the rules in the classroom.

▶ Invite your child to play games that involve a few simple rules. These can include made-up games or board games. Try to keep the experience positive so that rule following isn't automatically associated with a negative experience.

Help your child have a healthy perspective about the role of rules in his life. After all, he's going to be encountering a lot of them.

Reflect, Revise, Revisit

As you help your child make up rules, find rules, and discuss them, try to focus on respect for the role rules play in our lives. Children can look at rules as black and white, right and wrong, without understanding their purpose. While this is a natural part of their development, you also want to help your child understand that rules have more meaning than just what you can or cannot do.

THAT LITTLE VOICE INSIDE YOU

Inside every child is a little voice that tells them when something isn't right. That's great, but learning to listen to this little voice takes time, practice, and attention. Self-regulation is the ability to know, deep down inside, when it is time to stop, time to change, or time to make a different choice. In a community of learners, it is important for each child to hear that little voice and then have the wherewithal to know it may be time to choose differently.

As a parent or caregiver, you need to learn to recognize whether or not your child is demonstrating the skill of self-regulation. Does your child keep pouring the apple juice into a cup even after it starts to overflow? Does she walk up to a tower of blocks and automatically kick it over? Does she talk loudly in the middle of a church service? Does she get excited and interrupt you every time you start to tell her a story? Does she get overly upset if she doesn't get her favorite color? If you have answered yes to some or all of these questions, then your child has not yet mastered or developed her skills in self-regulating.

As a parent or caregiver, you should also know that self-regulation isn't always a problem of discipline or poor behavior. Instead, it is a skill that involves trial and error, reflective thinking, and decision-making that needs to be nurtured and taught.

What Your Child Should Know

Your child should know how to recognize when something she is doing or saying (or is about to do or say) just isn't right and that it's time to make a different choice.

How You Can Help

One of the best ways for young children to develop their skills in self-regulation is through play. As children play, they sometimes break the rules of play and cause someone to get upset or hurt. In most cases, when one child starts to get upset the others all stop what they are doing to see who is going to get in trouble, or they try to fix the situation on their own. The more children can work through an unhappy situation on their own and find a happy place, the better they are developing a sense of right and wrong and their ability to self-regulate.

There are three steps you can take to help build positive self-regulation skills:

▶ When play is interrupted by a problem that you need to step in and help with, begin with having the children *recall* what happened—what happened and why did it happen?

▶ Next *review* what other choices could have been made to keep the situation from going sour.

▶ Now try a little *role-play*: Act out the situation just as it happened before only this time making different choices. Role-playing with the children can help demonstrate positive communication skills and positive decision-making skills.

Let's give a quick example: Suzie wanted the red paint but Sally was using it. Suzy reached for the red paint cup but Sally quickly tried to move it out of Sally's reach and it spilled all over the floor—uh oh! This made both Suzy and Sally cry and now they both have your attention!

What to do? Recall what happened by asking Suzie and Sally to tell their stories. Review with Suzie and Sally other choices that could have been made. Role-play the events that just took place together only now, with your help, apply the other choices you just discussed. Hopefully this time you won't end up with paint all over the floor.

Make the role-play fun and upbeat instead of stern and serious. It's purpose should be to help Suzie and Sally learn how to make better decisions but also discover that it is so much more fun when they make better decisions.

Now that everyone is feeling happy again and knows what kind of decisions are good decisions, it's time to recruit two happy little girls to help you clean up the paint!

Reflect, Revise, Revisit

As a parent or caregiver, one of your responsibilities is to recognize teachable moments. Each one will be different and require you to assess the situation from a perspective of building self-regulation so that ultimately your child is making his own good choices without needing you to intervene in the process.

TO TELL OR NOT TO TELL

For many children it's a challenge to learn the difference between being a tattletale and bringing a legitimate concern to the attention of the teacher. This requires some advanced thinking. It can also be a challenge for you to help your child to know the difference.

What Your Child Should Know

Your child should know the difference between being a tattletale (the habit of telling on his peers without good reason) and being responsible (telling a teacher, parent, caregiver, or another trusted adult about something that is causing worry or concern).

How You Can Help

Helping your child to know when he should tell you about something, and when that's not necessary, is primarily a process of redirecting your child as the situation comes up. Here's a simple and fun way to help you redirect your child so he learns the difference:

▶ Create a tattletale box. Gather up a rectangular tissue box, some big googly eyes, and any other decorative bits and pieces you can lay your hands on. The more creativity you put into decorating the box, the more interested your child will be in playing along. You might make the box look like a robot or a monster or some other character your child is interested in or is familiar with. Be sure to keep the hole (or mouth) in the top of the box open.

After your tattletale box is completed give it a name. You might call it a "tattletale robot," for example. To learn more about making a tattletale box, check out the Tattle Monster by Giggles Galore! (*www.gigglesgalore.net/tattle-monster*).

Whenever your child is being a tattletale, send him over to tell his tale to the tattletale box. But whenever your child comes to tell you something that is necessary and warrants your attention, explain to your child why you appreciate his coming to you and then address the situation.

Reflect, Revise, Revisit

Tattling is often a way your child seeks attention. If you notice that he is persistently coming to you to tell on others, use the tattletale box to help curb the habit. At the same time, make the effort to respond to your child in other situations that will help him know that he can get your attention through more positive interactions. If you notice your child has a tendency to never tell you (or other trusted adults) something that really should be shared, encourage him to speak up. Your child needs to know that when he has a genuine need or concern it is okay and important to tell.

CHAPTER 8

The Larger Community

Beyond kindergarten is a broader community to which your child belongs. It's important that she feel a part of this community and learn about the others who help it function. This sense of community goes along with an understanding that not all people are the same. An appreciation for the differences among people will help your child be prepared to accept others and feel confident playing and learning with all kinds of children in her kindergarten classroom.

PEOPLE WHO HELP

As your child enters kindergarten, she will meet new people such as her teacher, school nurse, and others who are there to help and serve the members of her learning community. Introducing your child to some of these people will help your child understand their role and feel more confident interacting with them in that role.

What Your Child Should Know

Your child should have a basic knowledge of:

▶ Different people that work in her community

▶ The roles those people play in helping others

How You Can Help

Getting an up close and personal look at different roles people play in helping others in your community is a terrific learning experience for your child. Here are some ways you might introduce your child to community helpers and some steps to plan for the experiences:

▶ Consider taking your child to visit a local fire station, police station, veterinary clinic, restaurant, post office, hardware store, and dentist's office. Choose places to visit that your child will find interesting and people to visit who in some way help others in their daily jobs.

▶ Before heading off to visit a place of business, be sure to call ahead. Ask if the community helper you are visiting can give you a tour of the facility or vehicles. Find out if there is a good time to come or if it is okay just to drop by. Finally, ask if there are any rules or considerations you need to keep in mind before coming for a visit.

► To prepare for your child's visits, help her come up with a list of questions for the community helper. You may wish to ask each of the community helpers the same list of questions so your child can compare the different ways they each help others. Keep the questions meaningful and related to what is important to your child.

► As a follow-up to your child's visits, have things to do at home that will give her the opportunity to find out more about these places. Perhaps set up a mini-doctor's office or create a tabletop fire station for play.

Reflect, Revise, Revisit

As your child acts out the experiences of visiting community helpers at home, you will be able to see what was meaningful and interesting to her. Build on those experiences through conversation, play, and creativity.

PEOPLE HAVE DIFFERENT THINGS

Your child already knows that people need food to eat, a home to live in, and clothing to wear. These are the most basic of human needs, but not all people eat the same food, live in the same kinds of houses, or wear the same kinds of clothing.

What Your Child Should Know

Your child should:

▶ Begin developing his awareness of how people can be the same or different in where they live, what they eat, and what they wear

▶ Know that all people have value no matter what they eat, wear, or where they live

How You Can Help

▶ While you are out and about in the community, encourage your child to notice the different kinds of homes that people live in.

▶ Look for children's books or magazines to share with your child that show the kinds of clothing people from different backgrounds and different places wear. These examples can come from his own community and from around the world.

▶ Introduce different kinds of simple foods or treats to your child, ones that are out of his normal routine and represent different cultures than his own.

As your child develops his awareness of the similarities and differences in homes, clothing, and food you can help your child develop an appreciation for those differences. Show him that that these differences make the world a more interesting and special place in which to live.

Reflect, Revise, Revisit

As your child notices the differences between his own life and the lives of others, listen to his observations and attitudes about those differences. Keep your door open to conversations about these differences so your child can verbalize his thoughts and develop healthy perspectives towards others.

PEOPLE ARE DIFFERENT

Not only do people have different kinds of possessions, they also can look different. As your child heads off to kindergarten, she will most likely meet other children whose skin, hair, or eyes are different. Some children will be bigger and some smaller. Some children may have other physical differences and need the aid of a wheelchair or hearing aid to help them function.

What Your Child Should Know

Your child should know:

▶ That not all people are made exactly the same

▶ That every person is special and deserves to be treated with kindness and respect regardless of how he is different

How You Can Help

Seek out opportunities for your child to build relationships with children who are from a different race or have different abilities.

► Spend time with grandparents and other extended family members to help your child build positive experiences with people who are different in age or size.

► Get involved in local groups that reach a broad range of children and adults from different races and abilities. This can help your child build positive connections and relationships with others who are different.

Young children can naturally build up fears or be a little apprehensive when they are around people different from themselves. As they build relationships that cross boundaries of race or physical differences, children develop healthier perspectives and appreciation for others regardless of differences.

Reflect, Revise, Revisit

As you and your child come into contact with children or adults who are clearly different from the people your child is used to spending time with, watch your child's reactions and talk to him about his feelings, sense of curiosity, and perspectives. As you take note of your child's reactions and perspectives, you will be better able to assess the kinds of ways you need to help him feel confident around others and accepting of them.

CHAPTER 9

The Great Outdoors

As young children spend time outdoors, they are better able to develop their awareness of the natural environment and the role they play in taking care of this environment.

THE THINGS THAT GROW

As your child heads off to kindergarten, she will be exploring plants and the role people play in caring for them. A variety of opportunities to explore plants both in the natural environment and at home will give your child meaningful experiences and help her to participate confidently in conversations and activities involving plant growth.

What Your Child Should Know

Your child should have a basic understanding of how plants grow and get nourishment from water, sun, and soil.

How You Can Help

There are many ways to introduce the life cycle of a plant to your child in a meaningful and hands-on way. Here are a few ideas to consider:

▶ Take walks through the woods or a park or even your yard. Invite your child to look for plants, trees, and other living things. Create a positive link for your child to remember between being with family and enjoying nature.

▶ Create a nature journal for your child to record her findings while on your walks. She can draw pictures or collect a few items from nature to save in the journal. Help your child to decide which plants should be left in the ground and which plants might be okay to bring home.

▶ If you have a flower garden or vegetable garden, invite your child to help you plant, weed, and water the plants. If you don't have a garden, consider buying your child a potted plant to water and take care of on her own.

▶ While caring for different types of plants in or around your home, use these opportunities to have conversations about how the life cycle of a plant continues, how seeds grow, how much water or sunshine a plant may need, and how your child can help the plant stay healthy.

Reflect, Revise, Revisit

As your child is helping to care for plants or taking nature walks with you, use this time to ask her simple, open-ended questions about her observations of plants and trees. Questions like "How do you think that flower will grow?" or "How do you think that tree got so big?" will open the door for conversation and help you evaluate her understanding of plants.

CARING FOR ANIMALS

In his kindergarten classroom your child will also explore a variety of animals and the role people play in caring for them. Real-life experiences and interactions will help your child make connections between home and school.

What Your Child Should Know

Your child should be able to:

▶ Demonstrate a basic knowledge of the names of familiar animals and the sounds they make

▶ Identify a few basic differences between different kinds of animals such as those that are wild versus those that might make a good pet

▶ Know a few basic differences between animals that live in the water and those that live on land

▶ Have a sense of empathy for animals and an understanding of the role of people in caring for animals

How You Can Help

There are many different kinds of opportunities for your child to gain a meaningful understanding of animals. Here are a few ideas to consider:

▶ Where possible, take your child on a fun family visit to a local zoo, farm, or animal shelter. This will help him build meaningful memories involving animals. While on your visit, help your child to understand how to treat animals and talk to them. Use the visits as an opportunity to identify the names of different kinds of animals, what they eat, and where they live.

▶ If you have a pet, give your child some basic responsibilities for caring for it: keeping the water bowl full or brushing your pet's fur once a week. Model kindness and respect towards your pet and encourage your child to treat it with gentle hands and kind words.

▶ Get your child a pet of his own to care for. However, do some research first on which types of pets will be appropriate for his age group. Some pets require lots of specialized care or a specific type of environment. Know what kind of pet will be the right fit for your home and family.

▶ If you are not up to having a pet in your home on a permanent basis, consider offering to care for a neighbor's pet one weekend or volunteering at a local animal shelter. See if there are opportunities to get your child involved in local community action groups that care for domestic animals.

As your child has opportunities to interact with a pet or to visit animals at a zoo, he'll begin to understand the differences among animals and what it means to care for them. He'll develop rich and meaningful information that he can build on in the kindergarten classroom.

Reflect, Revise, Revisit

Anytime your child is around animals, watch how he interacts with them. Notice if he seems to have any fear or concerns about them and if he understands how to hold, pet, and care for them. Finally, ask your child open-ended questions that invite him to tell you what he is recognizing, remembering, or noticing about the animals that he encounters.

RESPECT FOR THE ENVIRONMENT

In the kindergarten classroom, your child will probably explore how to respect and take care of the natural environment. You can begin helping her learn how to care for the natural environment by developing healthy environmental habits at home.

What Your Child Should Know

Your child should know:

▶ A few basic ways that she can help take care of the natural environment

▶ What terms like *recycling* and *littering* mean

How You Can Help

Every household produces a variety of trash. If you haven't yet learned the difference between which trash is recyclable and which isn't, then it is time for you and your child to do a little research together.

▶ If you have Internet access, you can research the different kinds of materials that can be recycled. As you are learning about these materials, you and your child can put together a mini-recycling set of boxes of your own. Label each box with words and photos so your child will remember which items go in which box.

▶ Ask your child to sort through the things she is throwing away and see if some of them can be sorted into the recycling boxes. Grouping different items into different boxes will not only teach your child how to care for the environment but the process will also give your child the opportunity to build valuable critical thinking and organizational skills.

▶ See if there is a local recycling plant that you can take your child to visit so she can see firsthand where the recycling materials go after they're collected and hauled away.

▶ Take your child to visit a garbage dump or even outside to smell old trash that has been left in the trash can too long. Use these kinds of experiences to help her understand how trash can ruin the natural environment. A garbage dump or smelly trash can is a good way to include all her senses in the learning process.

When your family goes on picnics or other outdoor family outings, be a role model for your child by picking up trash. Take your child on a garbage can walk and help her notice where trash should be taken and where it should not be left. Talk about the animals and the plants and ask your child open-ended questions that lead to discussions on how a trashy environment might affect her way of life.

Reflect, Revise, Revisit

Through simple and natural interactions, you can begin to assess your child's understanding of terms related to taking care of the natural environment and of her role. By building a mini-recycling center of boxes at home, you will be able to observe your child's awareness of the recycling process and recycling materials. Keep the process simple and manageable so that she develops healthy habits and finds recycling something she can easily achieve. There are lots of ideas on how young children can learn to recycle available online at Planetpals! (*www.planetpals.com*).

PART III

Building on the Things to Know

As you help your child get ready for kindergarten, you will most likely ask yourself, "What kinds of things does my child have to know before heading off to school?" The answer begins with understanding the importance of building a strong foundation for learning. This in turn starts with hands-on, meaningful, and playful experiences that promote cognitive awareness, new understanding, problem solving, and critical thinking skills in content areas such as science, math, art, language, reading, and writing. Your child will then build on these experiences to learn the things he needs to know. To help you create a strong foundation for learning, we'll begin by introducing the basic core concepts of color, shape, number, and letter recognition, followed up with practical and meaningful strategies to help you foster your child's skills and abilities in all content areas of learning.

CHAPTER 10

The Core Concepts

The ability to recognize and differentiate between different colors is fundamental in all content areas of learning. Colors are one of the most basic ways young children observe and make sense of their world. Colors are used to help young children learn elementary math skills such as sorting and patterning and science skills such as organizing and classifying. As young children learn to recognize colors, they are also building skills that down the road will be used to help foster reading and writing.

Number recognition and counting are two of the most basic skills involving the use of numbers. When integrating the use of numbers and the process of counting with real-life objects and experiences, your child will develop a lasting knowledge and meaningful understanding of counting and number recognition.

Shapes are another core concept and serve many of the same learning goals as colors. Shapes are all around us, but for adults, shapes in the everyday world can be easily overlooked. Sometimes it is necessary to slow down and look at the world through a child's eyes. By paying more attention to everyday shapes that are present in your child's indoor and outdoor environment, you will be able to help your child draw connections between the name of a shape, the lines and curves of a shape, and the kinds of meanings or significance each shape has in the real world.

COLOR RECOGNITION

Color recognition is the ability to tell the difference between colors and to identify each color by name.

What Your Child Should Know

Your child should be able to:

► Comfortably distinguish the differences between the primary colors red, yellow, and blue

► Have a good grasp on the secondary colors of green, orange, and purple (violet)

► Verbally identify each of the primary and secondary colors in context of real-life observations and meaningful experiences

How You Can Help

Your child's ability to recognize colors isn't just about memorizing colors but also about having a rich and meaningful understanding of color. There are many ways to foster your child's recognition of color, but here are few ideas to get you headed in the right direction:

▶ Introduce color through hands-on creative activities and materials. As your child freely explores different colors of paint, markers, stamps, play-dough, and other materials, he will begin to develop his interest and appreciation of color.

▶ Introduce color to your child through engaging experiences such as reading a picture book together, building with colorful blocks and tubes, sorting through a basket of colorful pom-poms, or weaving a paper plate with different colors of yarn. Keep the process of color recognition hands-on, interesting, and engaging.

▶ Provide your child with sensory experiences that involve color. Young children remember best when they use all their senses to learn new concepts. Add color to a tub of water, shaving cream, or sand. Invite your child to help cook up colorful pancakes or add colorful icing to a cupcake. Provide opportunities for him to explore, mix, and build on meaningful experiences surrounding the use of color.

As your child participates in meaningful and engaging experiences involving color, facilitate conversation with him. Talk to him about his choices in color. Build on his experiences to draw attention to the differences in color and the names of each color, as well as how combining some colors helps create others.

Reflect, Revise, Revisit

Assessing color can be as simple as holding up a colored card and asking your child to tell you what the name of the color is. But the best way to watch your child's progress is through real-life experience. As you take a walk outdoors, talk to him about the colors he sees. Listen for his ability to describe his world or art or clothing in terms of color and build on his natural interest and shared knowledge.

ROTE COUNTING

Rote counting is your child's ability to count in numerical order starting at one and going up to ten or higher— depending on your child's readiness, interest, and experiences in rote counting.

What Your Child Should Know

Your child should be:

▶ Able to count verbally from one to ten

▶ Showing an interest in and making an effort to count beyond the number ten

How You Can Help

Rote counting is really just a matter of practice but that practice will be more fun for your child if you integrate the process through daily life experiences. Here are some examples:

▶ As your child walks up a set of stairs, invite her to count each step along the way.

▶ As your child is riding in the car with you, sing simple songs or rhymes that involve the counting process such as "One, two, buckle my shoe."

▶ While making a bowl of pudding, invite your child to count the number of times you are supposed to stir until the pudding starts to set. That is the easy part—counting how many seconds until it is time to eat the pudding is another story.

▶ Play games such as hide-and-seek. Invite your child to close her eyes and count to ten while you hide an object somewhere in the room. Teach your child how to play hide-and-seek with other children so everyone takes a turn counting and hiding.

Reflect, Revise, Revisit

Assessing the ability to count by rote is as simple as asking your child to start at one and count as high as she can go. However, the true measure of a child's ability to count up to ten and beyond is when she can demonstrate the same ability while engaged in real-life interactions and experiences.

COUNTING OBJECTS

Counting objects and rote counting are two different kinds of skills. Counting objects involves the ability to count by rote, but it also involves critical thinking skills.

What Your Child Should Know

Your child should have a basic working knowledge of:

▶ How to organize objects

▶ How to count objects and sets of objects

How You Can Help

Integrating the process of counting objects into daily life routines and fun experiences will keep numbers interesting and meaningful to your child. Here are some creative ways that you can encourage him to put counting into practice:

▶ Ask your child to count out five potatoes for potato soup or five seeds to plant in a pot or three scoops of food for the dog. Give your child specific tasks that involve counting out simple numbers of objects.

▶ Set up counting games for your child to play. For example, play games that involve the use of dice or counting spaces on a game board. You can make up your own games with dice and pom-poms or play games you buy from the store.

▶ Invite your child to count the number of big trucks he sees while you're driving down the road or the number of turns you have to make while traveling from one place to another.

▶ Help your child build collections of objects that he finds interesting. For example, your child might build a special collection of rocks, cars, or dolls. As he assembles his collection, express an interest in how many objects he has managed to collect. Invite your child to count out the objects in his collection and share with you how many he has managed to collect so far.

Reflect, Revise, Revisit

You can hand your child ten objects and ask him to count them, but you'll get a better idea of his ability to sort, organize, and count objects by observing him at play or by interacting with him through games or during rides in the car. Building a solid foundation for mathematical thinking needs to be a natural part of real-life daily experiences for your child so he will find the process achievable and meaningful.

NUMBER RECOGNITION

Number recognition is your child's ability to recognize numerical symbols such as 1, 2, 3, 4, and so on. Number recognition is different from counting numbers, although ultimately the skills of rote counting and counting objects will be combined with the recognition of numerical symbols.

What Your Child Should Know

Your child should be able to recognize the numbers 0 and 1 through 10. Having a strong, real-world ability to recognize the first ten numbers will give your child a solid place to build on as he is showing interest or readiness to move on to the combination of numbers 11, 12, 13, and above.

How You Can Help

Integrating numbers into your child's natural environment will build meaningful opportunities for her to interact with those numbers. Here are a few examples:

▶ Keep a set of magnetic numbers on your refrigerator for your child to arrange and rearrange. Use the numbers to play games with your child like "I Spy a Number" or make conversation about numbers while you are preparing dinner.

▶ Read simple books with your child that involve the creative use of numbers. Choose books that are about topics she'll find interesting and fun to read.

▶ While you drive to and from the store, invite your child to shout out numbers she sees on mailboxes, license plates, or signs.

▶ Give your child interesting tools to explore such as a calculator, ruler, scales, old telephones, and other tools that involve the use of numbers. Be sure to keep out paper and pencils for your child to "record" her own numbers while using the tools for play.

▶ Invite your child to help you measure out the ingredients for baking cookies or set out measuring cups and a tub of water so she can explore the numbers on the cups while enjoying the water play experience.

Reflect, Revise, Revisit

You can test your child's number abilities by holding up cards with the numbers 1 through 10 and asking her to tell you what each number is. However, as always, real-life observation will give you a truer assessment. While observing your child at play or while playing games or baking cookies with her, take note of her ability to read the numbers on the game or the measuring cups. Look for additional opportunities to help her recognize and remember numbers through everyday interactions.

ONE-TO-ONE CORRESPONDENCE

One-to-one correspondence in its most basic form is defined as your child's ability to match one object to a different object or number. The term has more complicated meanings, but for helping your child prepare for kindergarten, we'll focus on your child's ability to match objects with numbers or numbers of objects.

What Your Child Should Know

Your child should be able to match a set of objects to a corresponding number. For example, your child should be able to count out five pom-poms and then place them on a card with the number 5.

How You Can Help

▶ **SIMPLE:** Invite your child to sort a pile of twelve buttons into individual cups of an egg carton; or to park five Matchbox cars in a paper parking lot with five spaces; or to find the missing match to a pair of socks in a basket.

▶ **MEDIUM:** Invite your child to match a set of common but small objects to a set of numbers on a deck of cards. The higher the number, the more difficult it will be for your child, so you might start out with low-numbered cards and gradually work your way up to higher-numbered cards.

▶ **ADVANCED:** While setting the table for dinner, ask your child to count out the number of spoons or forks you will need at the table; then go and set the forks and spoons next to the plates. Your child will be exploring the process of matching the correct number of forks or spoons with the number of plates on the table. If he doesn't bring enough forks or spoons to the table, then he'll see that he needs to go back and get more forks or spoons.

Give your child opportunities to explore the process of matching numbers to objects; then allow plenty of time and space to self-correct when something doesn't fit just right.

Reflect, Revise, Revisit

You can best judge how your child is progressing with one-to-one correspondence when you watch him playing or while he takes on different tasks that involve counting. While observing your child, take note of his attitude. Does he seem to give up when things are not going well? Or does he work to solve the problem? If he's giving up, then simplify the kinds of tasks you invite him to do. Keep the process achievable, fun, and appropriately challenging so that your child will believe in his abilities.

Finally, always keep in the back of your mind that the best way to build confidence in mathematical thinking is by keeping the processes of building math skills fun, meaningful, and achievable. Remember that your child will not necessarily understand that setting forks out on a table is a mathematical skill. It isn't necessary to point that out to him. Instead, you are seeking to help him use daily life experiences to build a strong foundation for mathematical thinking as he heads off to kindergarten and beyond.

SHAPE RECOGNITION

Shape recognition is the ability to discriminate between different shapes as well as the ability to identify many of those shapes by name.

What Your Child Should Know

Your child should be able to:

▶ Tell the difference between simple shapes such as a circle and a triangle

▶ Identify many common shapes by name

▶ Recognize triangles, squares, circles, rectangles, ovals, octagons, diamonds, stars, and hearts

How You Can Help

Your child already knows different objects are different shapes. The trick is to match shapes with their names. Here are some ways to promote your child's recognition of shapes:

▶ A sandwich is not just a sandwich, but it is an opportunity to promote shape recognition through all of a child's senses. Cut your child's sandwich in half and then help your child recognize that this sandwich isn't just a sandwich but it is now two triangles. You can help your child notice that the sandwich has three sides and three corners, but as your child bites off one of the corners, say, "Oh, no! The sandwich isn't a triangle anymore!" Tomorrow's surprise sandwich may be a smelly peanut butter rectangle or a yummy ham square, but your child will have to wait and see what the shape will be.

▶ Shapes can be found hidden in all kinds of places both indoors and outdoors. A stop sign isn't just a sign but an octagon with eight perfectly equal sides; a door isn't just a door but a rectangle with two long edges and two short edges. What would happen if the door were round? Would you be able to shut it? Use questions not only to help your child identify different shapes but also to facilitate conversation and understanding about why each shape has a purpose in its design.

▶ The more hands-on your child can be with shapes, the better he'll understand the relationship shapes have to one another: building with differently shaped blocks or other toys, painting with different shaped sponges, sewing around cardboard shapes, sorting different sizes and shapes of buttons into a set of cups, and cutting playdough with cookie cutter shapes are all different ways your child can learn to recognize and differentiate shapes.

▶ As your child shows an interest in drawing different shapes, you can build on this interest by setting items on the table to explore and draw. For example, after spending time outdoors, don't come back inside empty-handed. Bring back a rock and set it on the table with crayons and paper. Invite your child to pick up the rock and examine it more closely, then use the rock as a source of inspiration to draw his own rocks, using simple shapes that the rock inspires. Perhaps your child's rock is more oval than round or perhaps it's a combination of smooth and pointed edges. Invite him to explore the shape of the rock and then to interpret the shape into his own drawing anyway he wants.

Finally, remember to use lots of language to help your child develop his awareness and familiarity with different shapes. Instead of just asking him to hand you a napkin, ask your child to please hand you a square napkin to go with your round plate that is sitting on your rectangular table. Okay, you don't want to go overboard, but try to integrate the language of shapes through everyday conversations and tasks.

Reflect, Revise, Revisit

Draw a set of shapes on a piece of paper, point to each one, and ask your child to name that shape. Get into the practice of noticing simple shapes while you and your child are busy running errands or while your child is building blocks. Reflect on your child's use of shape language when he is describing a picture or sign. Ask him questions that will direct his attention toward different shapes and then reflect on whether or not your child seems to be connecting the dots.

CHAPTER 11

Now I Know My ABCs

Just as with the other skills your child has been learning, writing is the foundation of many other areas of learning. In this chapter we'll look at the basic literacy skills your child should have on his first day of kindergarten.

ALPHABET

The alphabet is a set of symbols that have meaning only when we form them into words. But learning to say or sing the alphabet is just the beginning step towards developing connections between letters and words—a step for your child into a whole new world.

What Your Child Should Know

Your child should be able to sing and say the letters of the alphabet.

How You Can Help

Here are a few ways you can integrate the memorization or learning of the alphabet into everyday play and interactions.

▶ The traditional alphabet tune is a good way to help your child memorize the letters of the alphabet in order, but singing the song is memorization more than a skill that has meaning.

▶ You can also help your child become familiar with the letters of the alphabet by inviting her to say the letters rather than just singing them. Create a simple alphabet rap for your child to rhythmically chant along with you as you drive down the road.

▶ Play an alphabet game with your child. You start by saying the first three letters of the alphabet; then your child says the next three and so on until you get all the way to letter *z*. The purpose is to get her thinking about which letters come next in the alphabet rather than just automatically recalling each letter without any real thought.

A sit-and-drill approach to teaching the alphabet has no real-world meaning to a child, and it can lead to a feeling that learning letters—and ultimately, learning to read—is just plain boring. Keep all processes connected to letter recognition and the learning of the alphabet fun and achievable.

Reflect, Revise, Revisit

As you sing or chant with your child, you will easily be able to tell which part of the alphabet seems to have your child stumped. No need to put up big red flags. Just use your reflection as an opportunity to be more creative and consistent in your approach to promoting your child's enjoyment and ability to sing and say the alphabet.

LETTER RECOGNITION

The ability to recognize the letters of the alphabet is an important step in the process of building a foundation for literacy. However, it still lacks meaning in terms of how letters play a role in your child's daily life so it is important for you, as a parent, to know that letter recognition is a part of the process toward building literacy, not an end goal.

What Your Child Should Know

Your child should be able to identify most, if not all, the letters of the alphabet in both uppercase [A, B, C] and lowercase [a, b, c] printed form.

There is often a temptation to introduce only the uppercase form of a letter with the idea that it is easier for young children to recognize, but you'll notice that the majority of letters in this paragraph and in your child's world are written in lowercase form. Keep the lowercase form of letter recognition as a natural part of the process and know that your child is capable of recognizing both.

How You Can Help

Remember that letter recognition is a process that takes time for young children to master. However, it is important to note that you don't want to turn letter recognition into a drill-the-skill type activity. Instead, you will want to keep it interesting, creative, fun, and achievable so that your child will feel successful. Here are a just a few ideas to get you started on helping your child develop the ability to recognize letters:

▶ Keep letters around the house within eyesight of your child. These will draw your child's interest to playing with them and invite opportunities to talk about them. Put a set of magnetic letters on the refrigerator, a set of foam letters in the bathtub, children's books down low in a basket or on a shelf, a set of letter stickers with paper on a table, or an alphabet poster on the back of your child's bedroom door.

▶ Your home is filled with opportunities to recognize letters as well. A back of a cereal box has letters that you can use to play games with your child while eating breakfast. For example, "I spy a letter *b* on the box—can you find the letter *b*?" Other opportunities to explore everyday print from around the house can include identifying letters on toys, posters, shoes, shirts, hats, mail, labels, and calendars.

▶ Make your own creative activities that invite fun exploration of letter recognition and that use of all your child's senses. These can include, sifting letters out of a tub of water, manipulating play-dough with letter-shaped cookie cutters, painting with sponge-shaped letters, finding and cutting letters out of a magazine, and decorating cardboard letters with objects that start with the sound of each letter. All these activities will help to build letter recognition and keep it fun and achievable.

Finally, remember to get outdoors to look for letters. You can find them on signs, buildings, trucks, license plates, and the list goes on. Use sticks to print letters in the dirt or sand and rocks to design letters on a path. By searching for letters everywhere, your child will connect them to real-world things and places they represent. Over time, you will begin to help your child draw connections between the recognition of letters to words and the objects they represent.

Reflect, Revise, Revisit

Assessing letter recognition can be as simple as holding up a letter and asking your child to tell you what it is. As well, reflect on your child's ability to recognize letters as you interact with him in everyday activities and settings. As he is able to connect letters with objects that have meaning, your child will be increasing his ability to recognize letters as well as developing context for which letters have meaning.

THE SOUNDS OF LETTERS

The sound of letters (phonemes) is your child's ability to recognize and make the sound that each letter of the alphabet represents. Letter recognition and letter sounds are two skills that are different and yet they can and should be naturally connected.

What Your Child Should Know

Your child should know:

▶ That each letter of the alphabet has at least one specific sound

▶ The sounds of letters that he uses often or is most familiar with (like the first letter of his name)

▶ How to make the sounds of letters

How You Can Help

▶ Put action to your use of letter sounds. For example, as you say the letter *D,* then "ddddddrop to the floor like the sound of *D*"; when you say the letter *H,* then breathe *h*ot air on your *h*and. By pairing the sound of a letter with an action, your child will begin to connect the two, which will help remind her what sound each letter makes.

▶ Build on the sounds of letters in your child's name. Young kids have a unique interest in learning all about the letters in their names, and the natural opportunity to focus on the sound of the first letter in your child's name will often come before any other letter you explore together.

Most importantly, read with your child. Reading aloud to your child is one of the best ways to put the process of letter recognition and sounds together. As your child develops her interest in reading with you, she will naturally begin to show an interest in wanting to read on her own. As she shows interest, point to a familiar or simple word in her book and draw your finger across the word as you say the sounds of the letters. Avoid spending long lengths of time breaking down words of a good book—keep the reading experience fun and interesting, but for books you read often with your child, feel free to take a minute to build on her interest in letter recognition and sound.

Reflect, Revise, Revisit

Just as with letter recognition, you could assess letter sounds by holding up a set of letters and asking your child to make the sound. However, this can be frustrating to a child who may feel more pressure to perform for you rather than to relax. Reflect on letter sounds with your child on a regular basis. As she is invited to make the sound of a letter while reading a book with you or while playing a game, you will be able to identify where your child can use a little prompting.

Letter recognition and sound will be something your child will explore more deeply when entering her kindergarten classroom. Having a good grasp of what it means to recognize a letter or make a letter sound will be a good foundation. No need to stress every letter and every sound of the alphabet. Keep the process of learning letters and sounds natural, interesting, and fun for your child so she'll enter the kindergarten classroom excited to learn more.

CHAPTER 12

It's All in a Name

The foundations for learning to read and write often begin with a child's name. For a young child, name recognition and writing are very personal and meaningful. A child's name is associated with a sense of identity and being special. To know how to read and write your own name is empowering, and prekindergarten-age children (and younger) naturally have a need to know how to write and recognize their own names.

NAME RECOGNITION

Name recognition often is the beginning step toward learning to read and write other words. It gives the child a good grasp of both the sound of her name and the written version of her name. If your child goes by a nickname at home, like Bella, but you plan to enroll her in school under a formal name, Isabella, then you have a few things to consider.

▶ Which name will your child go by at school and is she familiar with that name?

▶ Which version of your child's name do you want her teacher to focus on?

▶ Which name will your child connect with while at school?

If you have chosen to use your child's nickname at home, then give her teacher a heads up. In any case, if she goes by one name at home but has a different name on enrollment forms and medical records, then it is a good idea to make sure your child is familiar and recognizes both versions of her name.

What Your Child Should Know

Your child should be able to:

▶ Recognize and respond to her name when someone familiar, like a parent, or someone not so familiar, like the neighbor next door, calls her name out loud

▶ Recognize her name in written form

To recognize her name in written form isn't the same as your child's being able to read or write her name. Instead, name recognition is being familiar enough with the combination of letters as a whole to recognize them as being her name.

How You Can Help

There are many ways you can help your child master name recognition. Avoid depending on the use of flash card drills because the reality is your child's name will show up at school in many different kinds of places, sizes, colors, and styles. Let's take a look at a few inviting and natural ways you can help your child with name recognition in the home environment.

(Keep in mind that when printing or displaying your child's printed name, the first letter should be a capital or uppercase letter and the remaining letters should be in lowercase form.)

▸ Display your child's printed name throughout the house: on the bedroom door, taped around a toothbrush, printed on a paper cup, or printed neatly on the inside of a favorite book. Integrate the written version of your child's name throughout your home so she will see it often in different sizes and in different places.

▸ Get creative and invite your child to make a name collage or a name puzzle to cut up and then put back together again.

As your child begins to master name recognition, she will also begin identifying specific letters, but for the purpose of name recognition, the goal is her ability to recognize her name as a whole word.

Reflect, Revise, Revisit

There are many fun ways to assess your child's mastery of name recognition. For instance, you might put a tag on every toothbrush and see if your child can pick out the toothbrush with her name on it. Add names to paper cups for each member of your family and see if your child can find the correct cup. Finally, you can play name games with your child. For example, play an "I Spy" game. Make sure your child's name is visible somewhere in the room and say, "I spy a big chair," then "I spy your name." As you spy each item, invite your child to see if she can find it, too.

As you play games or create opportunities for your child to pick his name out of a mix of others, you will not only be keeping the process fun and inviting but you will also be able to assess his progress in recognizing her own name.

MAKE YOUR MARK

When your child first begins the writing process, it can look like he is simply making marks on paper. Upon closer examination you will discover that those marks have meaning to your child. Mark-making can begin as early as three and is the beginning of attempting to write letters or numbers. Since the process of mark-making is an important step in a child's writing progress, it should be something your pre-kindergarten-age child is already demonstrating. Let's take a closer look at mark-making so you can identify where your child is in his development as well as, ultimately, the writing process.

What Your Child Should Know

Your child should be:

▶ Demonstrating an interest in mark-making

▶ Developing an interest in printing at least the first letter of his own name (which is often referred to as "making his mark")

This beginning step at mark-making or printing may look funny to you and be barely or perhaps even unreadable, but this is normal. A letter in a child's name (or his mark) can appear in many forms and find its way in random places and directions on paper or other writing surfaces.

How You Can Help

By experiencing a variety of mark-making activities your child will continue to develop his fine-motor skills (strength and ability to hold a writing tool) as well as his eye-hand coordination (ability to control the direction of the writing tool). Remember, the process of learning to write is a combination of fine-motor strength and development combined with the opportunity to freely explore the mark-making process. Here are a few ways you can foster a child's interest in mark-making:

▶ Offer him a variety of different types of writing tools such as markers, pens, pencils, dry-erase markers, chalk, and crayons. As he changes the type of writing tool for mark-making, he'll find new interest in making his mark!

▶ Offer your child a variety of surfaces to write on around the house such as paper (with and without lines), notepads, receipt books, a dry-erase board, a chalkboard, a blank book, paper on a clipboard, sticky notes, and envelopes. As you change the type of writing canvas for mark-making, he'll become more creative in his output.

▶ Look for additional opportunities and tools for mark-making in the child's natural world such as writing with a chalky rock on a driveway or writing with a stick on a sandy beach. Even leaving a mark with muddy fingers on a piece of wood still counts as mark-making.

▶ Make your own marks. Let your child catch you doodling at the table or drawing lines on a map or circling ads in a newspaper. He may ask to try too, so have an extra pen or pencil handy for him to join you.

▶ When your child draws a picture or gives his grandma a card, invite him to "write his name" or "make his mark" on the picture or card so everyone will know who created this wonderful piece of work.

▶ Positively acknowledge your child's mark-making and *never* be critical. Your child's confidence in mark-making, and ultimately writing, needs space and time to develop. As you show your enthusiasm for efforts made in mark-making, your child will be enthusiastic also.

▶ Don't rush out to buy workbooks and tracing paper. One sure-fire way to spoil a young child's interest in writing is to overly structure the process. If your child asks for a workbook, feel free to get one but still remember that he may use the entire workbook to make marks at this point.

Finally, remember that encouraging mark-making is part of your role. When you see something that reminds you of a letter or number or shape in your child's mark-making, offer up an enthusiastic response: "Hey, I see a letter *J* starting to take shape here!" or "I am enjoying looking at all these letters you have written on this paper." Or "I am so amazed at how much time you took to write out all these words." Look for specific efforts you see in your child's process of mark-making and offer up positive comments on those efforts.

Reflect, Revise, Revisit

Every single mark made by your child can begin to have meaning. Your role is to begin looking for the meaning behind the marks. There are several ways you can do that. The next time you find a piece of paper left behind by your child, examine the paper and look for signs of mark-making. You can (and should) assume that your child's marks have meaning. Ask your child to tell you the story his marks have to tell.

Collect those random pieces of mark-makings you find around the house and create a portfolio for your child. Invite him to continue to add to it. Every so often, take a few minutes to scan through the marks your child is making and see if you are starting to see signs of recognizable letters or shapes or other symbols you hadn't noticed before.

NAME WRITING

The step following mark-making is letter writing, creating symbols that are recognizable to you and to your child. Young children often make the most progress writing the letters in their name before writing any others. As mentioned in the section on name recognition, a young child is interested in writing her own name because it has meaning to her and she feels a great sense of pride when she can write her name all by herself.

What Your Child Should Know

Once your prekindergarten-age child has a good grasp of name recognition and mark-making, she should:

▶ Start to show interest in writing the letters in her name

▶ Be able to identify each of the letters in her name

▶ Begin to try writing each of the letters in her name, particularly the first letter

How You Can Help

Name writing can and should happen at the child's pace, but there are things you can do to help foster it.

▶ Keep your child's printed name visible around the house and invite her to notice the letters in her name. Your child may even ask how to spell her name. Use this as an opportunity to demonstrate and encourage her to try and write her name.

▶ As mentioned earlier, create a writing center (a designated place for coloring and writing and creating) for your child. Keep a variety of writing tools and paper there. Add a card with your child's name clearly printed on it to the writing center for quick reference. Anytime she needs a little help remembering what the letters in her name look like, remind her to take out the name card and look it over.

▶ Be a model for name writing. Let your child see you writing her name and invite her to help you with it on things such as birthday cards, Valentine's Day cards, and thank-you notes. Remember to model your child's name in the correct form: a capital letter followed by all lowercase letters.

▶ Encourage your child to print her name on drawings, paintings, pictures, and other things she has made before putting them up on the refrigerator or away in a folder. Don't be surprised if she asks you to do it for her—just encourage her to write at least the first letter of her name and gradually add a few more letters over time.

Finally, always look for ways to make the writing process more interesting and creative. For example, try pouring a small amount of salt in a shoebox lid or placing a small amount of paint on a tray and then invite your child to use her pointer finger to write in the salt or a cotton swab to write in the paint. See these two links for additional information on Salt Tray Writing (*www.teachpreschool.org/2012/03/writing-in-salt*) or Paint Tray Writing (*www.teachpreschool.org/2011/09/paint-and-write-boards-for-preschoolers*).

Reflect, Revise, Revisit

If you have already started a portfolio for your child's mark-makings, you can now add samples of your child's name writing. Review the samples over time and make note of the progress you see. Don't expect significant progress in a short time, but do look for consistency in effort over time.

Although you should continue to model the child's printed name correctly, don't be alarmed if she prints the letters of her name in random order, backward, or prints each letter in random places around the paper. At this stage of the name-writing process, you are looking for evidence that your child knows what letters are in her name and is attempting to put them in print—no matter which direction the name ends up going.

CHAPTER 13

Ready to Read

Your child will begin the path toward developing reading skills once he enters the kindergarten classroom, but to help your child get ready for reading, there are several ways you can promote the reading process at home. Before jumping ahead to the process of promoting reading, there are a few things to consider.

Reading aloud to your child in the comfort of your own home is by far the best way to get your child ready to read and interested in the reading process. Reading together should be a relaxing experience that you both enjoy rather than a frustrating or boring experience that you or your child feels that you *have* to do.

Choosing quality books that your child finds interesting is an important part of building a love for reading. Educate yourself about children's books and look for books that will capture your child's attention, tell a compelling story, include fun or interesting use of language and rhyme, challenge your child's thinking, and leave her asking you to read the book again.

When choosing a book to read with your child, pay attention to its length and the combination of illustrations and words on each page. Search for books that you think will hold your child's attention from beginning to end. In some cases, shorter books or books with more pictures may be better than longer books or books with lots of words on the page. In other cases, the length of the book will not matter because the story is engaging and interesting. Your child's interest in reading or your ability to keep her engaged in the story will depend on your individual style or your child's interests.

Reading a book more than once is a very good thing to do. If your child loves a particular book, feel free to read it often and look for other books that capture what she loves about this book.

Set aside a special time for reading with your child. Perhaps spending a few minutes before bedtime or right after dinner would work for you. Create a cozy place so that this is a meaningful and bonding experience rather than a "school activity." Building good memories related to reading helps to build a good attitude about it.

Finally, remember that reading isn't an overnight process or something your child must already know before heading off to kindergarten. It's a process that you can promote at home by building your child's love for reading along with a few readiness skills that will help your child be successful in the process of learning to read.

TAKING A PICTURE WALK

There are different methods of reading that you can explore with your child. One of the simplest is a picture walk.

What Your Child Should Know

Your child should know that each illustration (or picture) on a page tells something about the story of the book.

How You Can Help

Choose a book your child will enjoy reading with you. For the purpose of a picture walk, it doesn't matter if the book has words or not, but a combination of pictures and words will help draw connections between the words on the page and the illustrations in future readings of the book.

▶ Introduce your child to the cover of the book and ask her to tell you by looking at the pictures what she thinks the book might be about. Tell her that you are going to go on a picture walk together and see how the pictures tell the story.

▶ Starting at the beginning of the book, invite your child to take a look at the illustrations on each page and share her thoughts about what might be happening in the story. Give her prompts by asking open-ended questions such as, "What does it look like the little boy is doing?" or "Why do you think the little boy is frowning?"

▶ As you continue, provide prompts where needed and use the illustrations to tell the story. Your child's version of the story may not resemble the actual story at all, but this is okay. Eventually, when you do read the story it will open the door for new thinking and conversations about the story.

A picture walk will help your child begin to draw upon the illustrations to tell a story. It will help her develop the skill of starting on the left side of the page and then moving to the right to see the story progress. A picture walk will also help her connect the words on the page and the illustrations and to see how they work together to tell a story.

Reflect, Revise, Revisit

As your child takes a picture walk with you, you will be able to reflect on your child's understanding of the reading process, her ability to navigate from the beginning to the end of a book, and her ability to verbalize and formulate her thoughts about what is happening throughout the story. See Reading with Young Children: A Picture Walk (*www.teachpreschool.org/2012/03/reading-with-young-children-a-picture-walk/*) for more details on taking a picture walk.

LEFT TO RIGHT

Learning to read includes developing the practice of starting on the left side of a single word, a set of words, or an open page in a book and moving your eyes across the letters, words, or page from the left to the right. The left-to-right reading process can be naturally introduced through your time reading together or taking picture walks.

What Your Child Should Know

Your child should know that a story in a book begins on the left side of an open page in a book and progresses to the right.

How You Can Help

Here are a few tips you can apply to help your child begin the practice of left-to-right progression.

▶ While reading a book with your child or taking a picture walk, as you read along casually point your finger to the left-hand side of the page and skim to the right side of the page. It isn't necessary to skim your finger across the page word by word. The intent is simply to draw your child's eyes from left to right as you read the story aloud.

▶ As your child is showing an interest in sounding out letters or words, you can begin to skim your finger across a word starting from the left and skimming to the right.

Whether sounding out letters on a cereal box, reading a good book, or exploring a little name writing, take a few seconds to point your finger to the left-hand side of the word, sentence, or page and invite your child to begin on the left and then "go that way" (to the right).

Reflect, Revise, Revisit

As you observe your child reading and writing, you will easily be able to evaluate your child's understanding of left-to-right progression. Avoid making a big deal out of the practice. Instead, keep presenting subtle reminders and demonstrate the practice while reading with your child.

STORYTELLING

Storytelling can come from your child's imagination, a past experience, or from reading a book. Having him say the tale out loud invites your child to relate the events of a story in order, going from what happened first, then next, and finally, last. Storytelling also invites your child to tell you his thoughts or ideas in a creative or interesting way. As your child is building his interest in reading, the ability to retell or tell a story will reinforce his understanding of content and his ability to communicate events in the order in which they happen.

What Your Child Should Know

Your child should:

▶ Know how to verbally share a simple story from his imagination.

▶ Be able to demonstrate some ability to retell a simple favorite or familiar story in sequential order.

Whether he's telling or retelling a story, the goal is not to get the story exactly right but rather to have a sense of the characters in the story, the events, and the order of events in the story.

How You Can Help

Here are some creative props that you can use to promote storytelling.

▶ **MAKE A STORYTELLING BAG:** Fill a paper or a cloth bag with different items from around the house with which your child is familiar. For example, you might fill your bag with a banana, apple, carrot, and a stuffed animal. Invite your child to take the items out of the bag and use them to tell a story. If she needs help, you can take turns telling the story as you each take something out of the bag. Read Telling the Story Right Out of the Bag (*www.teach preschool.org/2011/09/story-telling-bag*) for more information on story telling bags.

▶ **PAINT A STORY:** Invite your child to tell a story in a painting. The painting may be nothing but lines and color, but hidden beneath those lines and colors may be a story your child wants to tell.

▶ **USE PUPPETS:** Invite your child to retell a familiar story with puppets or make up a story using puppets.

▶ **READ BACK:** Read a short story to your child and then invite your child to "read the story" back to you. Your child will retell the story by looking at the pictures and recalling the words of the story you just told.

▶ **BUILD A STORY:** Set out blocks, small toys, and other items to use for telling stories through play and construction.

▶ **DRAW A STORY:** Give your child a blank sheet of paper or a blank book to begin drawing and collecting her own stories. As she tells you the story hidden behind the drawings, print the words your child says and add a date so you can save the stories as a keepsake.

Storytelling is part of developing the skill to communicate ideas and should integrate creative, hands-on, playful experiences.

Reflect, Revise, Revisit

As your child spends more time telling and retelling stories, you will be able to observe her ability to express thoughts and ideas in a sequential order as well as her understanding of the events and concepts within a story.

Use these observations to encourage your child and build her confidence in her ideas and ability to communicate those ideas.

TAKING CARE OF BOOKS

With all of this talk about reading and enjoying books with your child, this is a good time to throw in how to take care of books.

What Your Child Should Know

Your child should know:

▶ That a book is something to be cared for and treasured

▶ How to take care of a book while reading it so that he can enjoy the book and so others can enjoy the book

▶ How to put a book back where it belongs when he's finished reading so that it will be ready to read on another day

How You Can Help

Giving your child ample access to books will inevitably lead to a few books getting stepped on or a few torn pages. It is important for your child to have plenty of access to books, and a sign of a well-loved book is when the pages get worn or a little torn around the edges. However, as your child prepares to head off to kindergarten, he needs to understand that reading books also comes with the responsibility to take care of them. Here are some ideas to help build responsible use and care of books.

▶ Designate specific places around your house where books can be put away. These might include a basket under the coffee table, a box in the toy room, or a shelf in your child's bedroom. Provide books in many different rooms throughout the house, and if there isn't a shelf or basket, then teach your child, at the very least, to pick the book off the floor and set it on a table when he's finished reading it.

▶ Keep an "Emergency Book Doctor's Kit" on hand for when pages get torn. Fill the kit with tape, erasers, cardboard, and anything else you can think of that might be appropriate to fix broken or torn books. Teach your child to come to you when he notices that a page in a book has been torn and needs to be repaired. When he is helping you tend to a "sick" book by taping up a torn page or erasing a pencil mark off of the page, he will begin to appreciate that the pages in a book are important.

▶ Model the care of books for your child by demonstrating your responsible use and care of a book. Talk to your child about why you can't leave a cup of water sitting next to your book on the table or why you use a bookmark rather than leaving the book laying wide open on the chair.

▶ After reading a good book with your child, hold your book as if you were giving it a hug as you sit and talk with your child about the book. This may sound silly, but hugging the book is a casual sign that you treasure it and the time spent reading it with your child.

Finally, give your child gentle reminders throughout the reading process about how to turn a page so it doesn't tear, or how to wash his hands so the pages of the book don't get sticky. Taking a few minutes to reinforce responsible use and care of books will help your child be a more successful and trustworthy book reader in his kindergarten classroom.

Reflect, Revise, Revisit

At the end of a day, notice where the books are in your child's room or reading areas. See if he needs to be reminded about how to put books away so they don't get ripped or stepped on. Consider if you need to provide new spaces to keep books organized and inviting. Sometimes, a messy book area sends the message that books are not meaningful or treasured. Take time to assess your child's book-reading environment and create the feeling that books are special and well loved in your home.

A PRINT-RICH ENVIRONMENT

So far, this section has focused on books, but it is important to note that getting ready to read goes beyond the pages of a book and extends into a child's environment as well. Where there are letters or words or messages to be read, new doors open to engaging your child in reading.

What Your Child Should Know

Your child should know that her world is filled with letters and words just waiting to tell her something.

How You Can Help

Make good use of words outside of books when introducing reading to your child. Here are a few ideas to help you do this.

▶ The next time you are at a stop sign with your child, draw her attention to the sign. Ask her to tell you what she thinks the message on the sign must say and why.

▶ As you are walking through a grocery store, take time with your child to notice the words throughout the store. Every word is trying to tell you something, whether it is a sign hanging from the ceiling, a number on the aisle, an exit sign over a door, or the ingredients list on a can of soup. Messages are all around us.

▶ At home, you can build a print-rich environment. Keep lots of different kinds of kid reading materials available in all areas of your home. Print words on a few index cards and strategically tape them around the house (chair, table, door). Keep your child's printed name accessible and visible throughout the house, and remember that cereal boxes, shampoo bottles, and other household items can all play a role in building a print-rich environment.

An exploration of print outside books can help to build your child's interest and excitement in reading. She'll realize that everywhere around her are messages that she can read.

Reflect, Revise, Revisit

One of the best ways to assess your child's awareness of print around her is to let her take the lead in the process. Listen to her observations about print on signs or buildings and use her comments as the basis of a conversation about what those words might say. If your child doesn't seem to be noticing the print in her environment, take the time to draw attention to it through fun and engaging conversations and experiences.

CHAPTER 14

Ready to Write

As your child begins the kindergarten experience, he'll explore the specifics of formal handwriting skills. For now, he can get ready to write through many different exercises. We've already talked about a few important writing-readiness skills such as fine-motor development and mark-making, but here are a few additional getting-ready-to write processes you can explore with your child.

LEFT TO RIGHT

Just like the reading from left to right practice we talked about earlier, you will want to encourage your child to develop the habit of writing from left to right. Keep in mind that it is not unusual for young children to write in all directions—especially when they begin to print actual letters. However, for this section, the focus is on "scribble writing" rather than writing specific letters in words or a child's name.

What Your Child Should Know

Your child should:

▶ Be able to produce scribble writing

▶ Begin on the left side of the paper and scribble to the right side

Although ultimately you want to encourage your child to write all letters and words starting on the left-hand side of the page and going right, for this section the focus is on "scribble writing." Scribbling or doodling messages across a piece of paper is considered an important part of learning to write. As your child scribbles a sentence, he should develop the habit of beginning on the left side of the paper and doodling or scribbling toward the right.

How You Can Help

Helping your child to write from left to right begins with your recognition of the value of scribble writing and doodling. When your child uses scribble writing as a way to write you a letter, make a list, or take notes, he is demonstrating the realization that symbols on paper have meaning and messages.

It is important not to refer to your child's doodling or scribble writing as "scribbling" when talking with him or in his hearing. Instead, accept scribble writing as part of the process and ask your child to share with you what his or her message has to say.

▶ Give your child ample opportunity and materials to foster his or her writing such as paper with or without lines along with crayons and markers. As you observe your child writing on paper or a chalkboard, encourage him to begin on the left side of the writing surface and write his message across the surface toward the right.

Reflect, Revise, Revisit

Take time to observe your child as he is writing or scribble writing a letter to you or a note on a clipboard. Notice if he's writing from left to right and, although you don't want to pester him, take time every so often to show him where to begin his notes and the direction to go from there.

JOURNALING

As your child enters kindergarten, she will most likely begin keeping a journal or a portfolio of writings. You can give her some experience with this.

What Your Child Should Know

Your child should know:

▶ How to open the pages of a journal (or blank book) and draw pictures, words, or other messages (scribble writing)

▶ How to use each new page of the journal for a new message or drawing

How You Can Help

As your child begins showing an interest in scribble writing or in drawing pictures for you that have an intended message she wants to share, introduce her to the process of putting some of those messages in a journal.

▶ Make a journal for her. It can be as simple as a spiral-bound notebook, a blank book, or a set of papers stapled together with a cover. Let her decorate the cover as she wishes.

▶ Make a second journal for yourself so that you can model keeping a journal and using proper writing form (left to right). The goal is not to dictate or model what to write or draw in the journal, but rather how to add an idea to one page at a time.

▶ After your child draws in her journal, see if she would like to read the message aloud or tell you about it. Print, as closely as you can, the words your child uses to share her message with you in the journal. Let your child see you printing those words and using good writing form.

▶ Feel free to introduce some interactive writing into your child's writing and drawing experiences. That is, begin writing or drawing something and then let your child take over and complete it.

Finally, you may wish to add a date to each of the writings or drawings in the journal.

Reflect, Revise, Revisit

As you go through your child's journal, you will begin to see different forms of drawing and writing take shape. You can use the journal as a guide to discover what words your child would like to write or what stories she enjoys drawing and sharing. You can promote her interest in journal writing best by keeping the journaling process open-ended and letting her choose her own content to add.

WRITING OUTSIDE THE LINES

Much, if not most, of your child's writing experiences in kindergarten will be with typical writing tools such as crayons, markers, and paper. As he is getting ready to write, you want to keep the writing process creative and inviting by extending it beyond the typical writing tools and experience.

What Your Child Should Know

Your child should find the writing experience to be creative, interesting, fun, and achievable.

How You Can Help

Invite your child to sample different kinds of writing opportunities. Here are a few examples of different writing opportunities.

► Writing on different surfaces such as on an easel, chalk-board, clipboard, and dry-erase board can keep your child interested in exploring the writing and drawing process.

► Writing in different types of material such as with a finger in a tray of salt or sand or writing in shaving cream or paint will keep the writing experience fun and engaging.

Offer a variety of writing tools and notice which ones your child seems to enjoy the most for drawing as opposed to writing. Different writing tools have different effects on paper, so be observant and make sure that the writing tools you are sharing with him are in good condition and work well for the kinds of drawing or writing he is exploring.

Reflect, Revise, Revisit

As your child explores writing outside the lines of paper and pencil, you can assess his interest in writing and drawing and his understanding of the writing or drawing process. If he's uncomfortable getting his hands messy, provide more nonmessy materials to use, like salt or sand. If your child loves to finger paint, though, give him more messy stuff (paint or pudding).

CHAPTER 15

Language

We all use language as a way to express our thoughts and ideas, wants and needs, and likes or dislikes. As your child prepares for success in kindergarten, she will need to have a good grasp of language.

VOCABULARY FOR LANGUAGE

Language consists of a broad set of terms or words commonly known as vocabulary.

What Your Child Should Know

Your child should:

▶ Be continuously developing her own vocabulary

▶ Use her vocabulary as a natural part of communicating in her everyday world

How You Can Help

As a parent, it is important for you to understand that vocabulary doesn't mean searching through the dictionary to drum up complex words for your child to memorize. Instead, your child's vocabulary should consist of words that have meaning in the context of the things she experiences or needs to know in order to communicate effectively in everyday situations. Here are some ways to help her increase her library of age-appropriate words.

▶ Read aloud often. Quality children's books are filled with words that have meaning to a young child. Read a variety, including books with words that rhyme, books about color, opposites, transportation, community helpers, zoo animals, and anything else that is of interest to your child. As she reads along with you, she will discover new words and their meaning in a way that is easy to understand and simple to integrate into her own language.

▶ Take your child on outings to a zoo, library, pumpkin patch, the woods, fire station, and other places that will help to introduce her to new words and experiences related to those words. As she experiences people, animals, nature, and places in an up close and personal way, she will draw on those experiences to learn, remember, and integrate new words into her own use of language.

▶ Introduce your child to new foods, materials, and tools. As she experiences the tastes of new foods or the use of new tools and materials, she will be developing a meaningful understanding of new words.

As well as introducing new experiences that build new vocabulary, encourage your child to "use her words" to communicate with you. Invite her to talk about experiences and use the new words frequently. Ultimately, your goal is to foster your child's ability to communicate with others by giving meaningful experiences with which to build a library of words.

Reflect, Revise, Revisit

As your child is telling you a story or asking you a question, pay attention to the words she uses to express her ideas, needs, wishes, wants, likes, or dislikes. If needed, give her the words to say and continue to provide experiences that will naturally build a vocabulary.

TOOLS FOR LANGUAGE

There are many tools to help promote language and the use of vocabulary that your child is exploring.

What Your Child Should Know

Your child should know how to use his words to express his ideas, needs, wants, likes, or dislikes.

How You Can Help

Here are a few tools that you can use to help your child with the process of building strong language skills.

▶ Puppets are a fun way to tell a story, act out a play, or sing a song because your child will have to use his words to make the puppet talk. You can make puppets from a paper bag or sticks, or pick up puppets at a store. Invite your child to read a story and then make his own set of figures to retell the story.

▶ Dress-up clothes and dramatic play draw in young children to explore the role of other people in their lives. As your child steps out of his own shoes and into those of Daddy, he will want to use language that Daddy uses. Dress-up clothes can include any kind of item that invites your child to play a role and can include second-hand clothes, old Halloween costumes, hats, scarves, capes, and shoes.

Any kind of tool for play that invites your child to put his thoughts and ideas into words can help him build his use of vocabulary and overall language skills.

Reflect, Revise, Revisit

As you observe your child at play or when he's talking to others, take note of his ability to communicate his ideas effectively through the use of words and language. If he becomes quickly frustrated when trying to express his ideas or words, then it's time to do a little detective work to see how else you can help.

CHAPTER 16

STEM

STEM is an acronym for the content areas of science, technology, engineering, and math. The goal of STEM in early childhood education is to build a foundation of meaningful and enriching experiences in each of these content areas through real-life experiences so that as young children enter their formal years of education (kindergarten and above), they will approach these areas of learning feeling competent and confident. Let's take a brief look at each of these content areas and see how you can help your child build her confidence and sense of competence.

I AM A SCIENTIST

Young children have a natural curiosity about their world—in many ways you could say they're natural scientists. Scientific exploration can provide amazing opportunities for developing skills in asking questions, making predictions, probing for answers, and building critical thinking skills in problem solving and decision making. A significant aspect of science in early learning is the development of new vocabulary. As your child experiences interesting opportunities to freely explore her world, you will be able to help her draw meaningful connections to words that evolve from scientific thinking and discovery.

What Your Child Should Know

Your child should know:

▶ That she is already a scientist

▶ That she is capable of asking questions, making predictions, testing and trying new things, and finding answers or solutions

How You Can Help

When you think of science, perhaps you're only thinking of test tubes and goggles and laboratories. Although this is one aspect of science, there is far more to science than this. For young children, science is the process of exploring their world with the intention of building new knowledge about the things in it. Your role is to be a facilitator of language, opportunity, and interest. Here are some ways you can foster your child's confidence in science.

▶ Offer opportunities for your child to freely explore different tools of science. For example, set up a table outside with magnifying glasses, scales, tweezers, plastic spoons, cups, water, paper, pencils, and a box. Invite your child to use the box to collect leaves, rocks, sticks, seeds, plants, dirt, or other items from nature, and then bring the items back to the table and examine them more closely. Suggest that she use the tools of science to explore the items from nature any way she wishes. She might want to pull seeds out of a plant with a pair of tweezers or weigh rocks on a set of scales or float leaves in a tub of water. Give her the freedom to use the tools as she wishes to explore the items she has collected.

▶ Do a little research on how different combinations of household products can create fun and interesting reactions. Gather the materials for your child to enjoy a little experimenting with you. For example, you can invite your child to mix vinegar, water, and baking soda to create wonderful bubbles or explore the properties of solid and liquid by making your own goop. Just pour two to three cups of water and a box of baking powder in a tub, then stick your hands in and play! As you swish the baking powder in the water it becomes a liquid, but if you try to scoop up a handful of baking powder, it will become a solid once again. There are many simple and safe household products you can explore. Remember always to monitor these kinds of activities and to do your research first so you can take measures to keep your child safe and provide her with boundaries or guidance as to responsible scientific exploration.

▶ Invite your child to begin any science exploration with a question and then invite her to follow up that question by making a guess about what the answer might be. Your child's question can lead to an entire unit of scientific exploration as you help her gather the materials needed to find the answer or solve a problem.

As your child explores her world, remember to use these opportunities to facilitate new language by talking with her about the process and materials she is using.

Reflect, Revise, Revisit

As your child explores her world, be an observer of her ability to ask questions, make guesses, and seek answers. Notice where you can help promote her natural curiosity and yet not take over the process.

I AM TECHNOLOGICALLY SAVVY

There is no question that today's kids live in a technologically driven world, and that it doesn't take long for young children to become tech savvy. In today's world when the word *technology* is mentioned, the first thing that comes to mind is a computer and the Internet. But technology also can include other devices such as cameras, video and audio recordings, overhead projectors, and iPods.

With the advancements in technology, there also comes a need for balance. Technology has a bad habit of keeping young children from experiencing outdoor play, messy art, and other important early learning processes. To keep technology in balance when it comes to early learning, you must use it as a way to supplement or extend hands-on, real-life learning. Never let it become a replacement.

What Your Child Should Know

Your child should:

► Have a basic set of skills and experiences, using a variety of technological tools

► Know that technology can be helpful in learning new things

► Know what the boundaries are for the use of technology in your home or away from home

► Know how to use technology responsibly and with care

How You Can Help

One of the first issues in promoting the basic use of technology items and setting boundaries for their use is to have access. If you do not happen to have a computer, camera, or other technological devices in your home, you'll want to find other places where you might be able to give your child opportunities to explore technology. A library or a friend's house will do. Once you have access to basic forms of technology, here are some ways you can extend (not replace) learning through its use.

▶ Whenever your child shows an interest in something (a book, an animal, in weather), invite him to use the Internet to research additional information. Sit with your child and use the Internet for a specific purpose. Model the use of tools such as the mouse or the keyboard and give your child the opportunity to use these tools under your watchful eye and helpful guidance.

▶ Invite him to take photos with a digital camera in order to make a poster, book, or slide show to tell a story about his day, a special event, or other interest he may have.

▶ Read and record a favorite children's book or sounds from around the house or outside to listen to on an iPod or other device. Let your child record his own voice telling a story or singing a song, then play it back for you to hear.

Remember to model and teach responsible use and care of technology and set boundaries for its use that will help your child use these devices in a balanced and constructive way.

Reflect, Revise, Revisit

As you observe your child's use of technology, consider additional ways he can be more independent with his use of it while at the same time remaining responsible and within your set rules. Remember, the goal of technology isn't to replace hands-on learning opportunities but to expand those opportunities.

I AM AN ENGINEER

Engineering may sound like a big word for early learning, but the planning, constructing, reconstructing, dismantling, and testing of how shapes and objects fit together or work together is something young children automatically do every day.

What Your Child Should Know

Your child should know:

▶ That she is capable of creating, building, and designing with simple to complex materials

▶ How to assemble and disassemble simple to complex puzzles, railroad tracks, blocks, and other toys or objects

▶ Basic differences among different kinds of lines, curves, and shapes

How You Can Help

Building your child's confidence and competence as a young engineer will require access to a variety of materials she can build with, manipulate, shape, put together, and take apart. Engineering materials can consist of store-bought toys such as Legos, blocks, waffle blocks, puzzles, and magnetos, but engineering doesn't have to come in a box. Engineering opportunities exist through homemade or natural opportunities as well. Here are some examples of homemade and natural engineering projects.

▶ Cardboard boxes of all shapes and sizes create wonderful tools for engineering. Your child can stack the boxes, balance them, cut out and create buildings with them . . . the list goes on.

▶ Items from the kitchen such as straws and toothpicks make wonderful engineering tools. Your child can use the straws to make shapes or chains, or use the toothpicks to create designs, lines, and patterns. Tape a few paper towel tubes together and you will be able to construct tunnels for cars or marbles.

▶ Items from nature are also wonderful tools for engineering. Your child can build with sticks, create games with rocks, and turn a tree into a fort.

▶ Find simple objects around the house that your child can take apart and try to put back together again. The items can include a flashlight or an old toy that no one plays with anymore.

Remember that engineering is the process of building, designing, creating, and taking tools from the everyday world to see how your child can manipulate, take apart, and put the objects back together.

Reflect, Revise, Revisit

Observe your child's natural curiosity in objects around and outside the house. Use your observations to facilitate the engineering process and then use the process to facilitate new language through conversation and questions.

I AM A MATHEMATICIAN

The goal of mathematical thinking in your child's early years is to build a strong foundation for a more formal math program once he heads off to kindergarten. The kinds of experiences that lead to a strong foundation include hands-on opportunities for the exploration of concepts such as weight, measurement, size, time, and numbers.

What Your Child Should Know

Your child should know:

▶ That he is capable and competent in math

▶ That each time he feeds the dog a cup of food or pours a glass of juice or matches up a pair of socks he is successfully using important math skills

How You Can Help

Your role is to be a facilitator of opportunity, curiosity, problem solving, and language as your child absorbs simple to complex mathematical ideas. Natural opportunities to help your child develop his mathematical skills and confidence are all around you. Here is a brief look at some of those opportunities for building a strong foundation for mathematical thinking.

▶ Cooking with your child offers an abundance of mathematical concepts. While cooking with him, facilitate conversation about common cooking processes such as measuring, stirring, pouring, and timing. Use questions to get him thinking and problem solving.

▶ Additional opportunities for math can include spending time in sand play or water play. Add tools for play that promote counting, measuring, filling, pouring, straining, and mixing to your child's play area.

▶ Help your child collect a variety of small items from outdoors or indoors that can be used for counting games, comparing, sorting, graphing, and patterning.

Reflect, Revise, Revisit

Introducing simple tools and processes that promote mathematical thinking will help you observe and facilitate conversation with your child. Through your conversations you can introduce new math terms such as "inches," "feet," "longer," "shorter," "higher," and "lower." Remember that mathematical thinking during the early years doesn't have to be complex—instead concentrate on making math interesting, inviting, and achievable.

CHAPTER 17

The Arts

One of the most valuable ways to build new skills and foster an interest in early learning is through the arts. As the arts are integrated throughout all content areas of education, learning remains fun and hands-on and young children are inspired and encouraged to use their imagination.

I AM AN ARTIST

Young children are natural artists. Their sense of curiosity and wonder gives them an uninhibited ability to express their views and to explore their world through artful experiences. Adults tend to want to control or shape a child's creative expression, which ultimately leads young children to doubt their ability to be creative. For young children, art is about the exploration of color, materials, and processes and not so much about making a finished product that everyone will recognize.

What Your Child Should Know

Your child should know that his ideas and interests can be expressed through art in a way that is self-satisfying and pleasing.

How You Can Help

Giving your child lots of opportunities to explore art through a variety of processes and materials will allow her to build her skills and confidence in the area of art expression. Let's take a look at the different types of materials and processes she can explore.

▶ She can have fun painting with many different materials and processes: sponge painting, easel painting, finger painting, printing with objects, painting on small or large canvases. She can add different textures or smells to the paint such as powdered drink mixes, salt, and shaving cream. Changing the texture, smell, painting tools, and painting canvasses can all lead to new experiences that will invite her to explore the creative process.

▶ Creating with different types of paper and glue is another form of art that young children can explore. Your child can tear or cut up newspaper, tissue paper, or construction paper and glue it together in a pattern or design.

▶ Creating with play-dough or clay is another way your child can freely explore the creative process.

▶ Creative art can also include creating patterns, designs, or collages with blocks, buttons, seashells, rocks, and other kinds of materials that are both natural and manmade.

▶ Change the location of art experiences. Take art outside or paint next to a window. Your child will find these new places will inspire new interest, ideas, and creativity.

Keeping the creative process open-ended will encourage your child to explore the materials, mix the colors, and express her own ideas through hands-on and interesting activities.

Reflect, Revise, Revisit

Refrain from pushing your own agenda for your child's creative experiences. Are you telling your child how to paint a flower, or are you giving her the tools and prompts to explore creatively? You might choose to set a flower next to your child's workspace to inspire her, but keep in mind that her version of the flower may not be what you expect. Keep your focus on being creative rather than the end result. This will help your child build confidence and enjoy the experience.

I AM A MUSICIAN

As your child enters the kindergarten classroom, he will most likely be introduced to different kinds of music and movement experiences. His class will sing and dance together as everyone listens and learns new songs or plays musical games. The children will listen to music as they paint or use music to help them sing and follow simple directions throughout the day.

What Your Child Should Know

Your child should know how to:

▶ Sing a simple song

▶ Make up new songs

▶ Play musical games

▶ Move to different musical rhythms and sounds

How You Can Help

Some children feel awkward singing new songs or moving to music and it takes them time to warm up to the idea, while others love to sing and dance and play musical games. As you seek to build positive attitudes about music and movement, here are some things to consider.

▶ Musical games can consist of playing games like musical chairs, "Ring-Around-the-Rosie," the musical freeze game, or children tapping rhythms with their hands. Playing musical games can be fun and engaging and will help your child learn to listen to music and rhythm and build positive connections with music.

▶ Use instruments to explore the sounds and rhythm of music as well. You can help your child engineer his own homemade musical instruments. For rhythm, make a drum out of a coffee can. For vibration, make a guitar by putting rubber bands around a shoebox lid. For sound, put some beans inside a small container with a lid. For pitch, add different levels of water to a set of glass jars and tap them lightly with a spoon. As your child explores the process of making and playing with musical instruments, he'll develop new appreciation for the vibration, rhythms, patterns, and sounds of music. See DIY Musical Strummies (*www.teachpreschool.org/2013/03/diy musical-strummies*) for more details on making a rubber band guitar, and see Balloon Bongo Rice Shaker (*www .minieco.co.uk/balloon-bongo-rice-shaker-guiro*) to learn how to make your own super cool bongo drums!

▶ Simple songs have wonderful rhymes, patterns, and language. Introducing your child to new songs will help him build confidence and introduce new language and language skills in the process of singing. Your child can also explore making up his own songs to sing.

▶ Putting words, concepts, or simple directions to music can help children build their memory bank of words and improve their listening skills. For example, singing the letters of your child's name to a familiar tune can often help your child remember the letters of his name. Singing a hand-washing song can help him remember the entire process of washing hands from soap to scrubbing to rinsing. Putting words into song motivates young children to listen more closely and helps them to remember more easily. Integrating music into the day will help to build your child's comfort level and confidence. Music and movement will help him build new skills in areas such as language, literacy, balance, patterning, and creativity. For many children, a well-rounded approach to the use of music in their daily lives makes them feel happier, more confident, and more at ease with themselves and with others.

Reflect, Revise, Revisit

Invite your child to sing and dance with you or play musical games with you. Be sensitive to individual feelings or attitudes about music. If he feels music is silly or if singing or moving to music makes him uncomfortable, then seek out new ideas that will build your child's interest, confidence, and love for the musical experience.

CHAPTER 18

A Healthy Experience

Part of success in kindergarten will depend on your child's health. A tired child has more trouble concentrating, getting along with others, and being flexible. A hungry child can be unreasonably emotional and unable to focus on anything. A child who doesn't get enough exercise or time outdoors can feel restless or lack the energy to make it through an entire day. Let's see what you can do to give your child a healthy and successful start in her new kindergarten classroom.

I NEED SLEEP

For young children, sleep is an essential part of success in kindergarten. A good night's sleep will help your child feel more confident, get along better with others, have better clarity of thought, and stay in a better mood throughout the school day. For many young children it takes a few weeks to get used to the new schedule and new demands. Your child may feel more tired than usual, and sleep will be an even more critical requirement for getting through each day.

What Your Child Should Know

As your child prepares to head off to kindergarten she should know that getting enough sleep at night is an important part of helping her feel good and do her very best in school.

How You Can Help

Here are a few ways you can help your child get a good night's sleep.

▶ Get into a healthy school night routine that includes dinner, bath, school work, and a little downtime for reading or quiet play before heading off to bed.

▶ Don't overload afternoons or evenings with extracurricular activities such as gymnastics or karate classes. Give time to adjust to the new school schedule.

▶ Make sure your child is getting between ten to twelve hours of sleep on a school night. Remember that includes Sunday nights.

Reflect, Revise, Revisit

If your child is having problems adjusting to going to kindergarten, making new friends, or following the rules, consider whether or not she's getting enough sleep. If she's having trouble sleeping, consider consulting with her doctor to see if there is something in her diet or routine that you may need to change.

I NEED NUTRITION

Eating a good breakfast before school and planning for healthy meals and snacks during and after school is an important part of helping your child have a successful school experience.

What Your Child Should Know

Your child should know that making good choices about what he eats throughout the day will help him feel stronger and happier in school. Research has shown that fruits and vegetables make good brain food!

How You Can Help

As your child heads off to kindergarten, your family may need to make an adjustment when it comes to meal times. The grocery bill might even go up a bit.

▶ Your child will most likely come home from kindergarten with a very hungry tummy so plan to have a variety of healthy snacks on hand that will curb his hunger, yet not spoil dinner.

▶ A healthy breakfast before school is a must. Your child needs to eat something before school that will help him sustain energy and make it all the way until lunchtime.

Reflect, Revise, Revisit

If your child is having trouble eating, doesn't seem to feel well after eating, or exhibits obvious changes in behavior or energy levels, from low to above-average energy, consult your doctor to see if there are any food allergies or other health concerns to be aware of and to manage.

I NEED EXERCISE

In the hustle and bustle of going to kindergarten, then coming home to do all the other daily routines, make sure there is time for outdoor play and exercise. These help young children to release stress, build strong muscles, and enjoy being a kid. The fresh air and sunshine that comes while young children are outdoors is good brain food, too. As the body gets moving and lungs breathe in fresh air, your child's brain is benefiting.

What Your Child Should Know

Your child should know that:

▶ Exercise is an important part of staying strong, healthy, smart, and happy

▶ Exercise means to get your whole body up and moving

▶ The best kind of exercise is to go outside and play

How You Can Help

Scheduling time for exercise into your daily routine is a must for young children. Here are a few ideas for getting her up and moving.

▶ Get outdoors every day and play. Whether it is running around the back yard, riding a bike, going to the park, planting flowers, or taking a walk together, you want to make sure your child is getting as much time in outdoor play as possible.

▶ When outdoor play isn't a possibility, come up with other plans for getting your child actively moving around the house. Dance to a fun children's song, hop on one foot, do some jumping jacks, or play simple games that get everyone up and moving. All these will help to keep your child feeling strong and healthy for school.

Reflect, Revise, Revisit

Stay aware of how your child spends his downtime after school. Look for opportunities to get him outdoors or up and moving indoors. Sitting around watching television or playing games on a computer may seem like a good way to relieve stress and relax, but these types of activity don't give the brain any rest at all. The best approach to a healthy brain is to get up, go outside, and actively play.

The Finish Line

READY FOR KINDERGARTEN

If you have been diligently putting into practice the ideas, concepts, and practices in this book, then you have been giving your child the tools he needs to be ready for kindergarten. There is always the worry that somehow you could or should be doing something more, so when the worry starts to sneak in, keep these points in mind:

▶ Your child is competent and capable, and as obstacles come up along the way, you will be there to provide the support and guidance she needs to make healthy choices and overcome obstacles.

▶ Your child is a unique individual with his own ideas, preferences, interests, and learning style. Meet your child where he is in this moment and recognize that every day your child is learning something new.

▶ Celebrate little or big accomplishments along the journey to kindergarten readiness with a hug or a high-five. Success comes as your child discovers and builds on her own strengths and abilities.

Remember that your prekindergarten-age child's job is not to act like a kindergartener or to do the work of a kindergartener. Instead, your child's job is to enjoy the prekindergarten years through hands-on exploration and play. Through these kinds of experiences, your child will be ready for kindergarten.

Index

O

P

R

About the Author

DEBORAH J. STEWART, MEd, is a wife, mother, and grandmother of two little boys. She holds a master's degree in early childhood education and has been teaching, writing, speaking, and training others for more than twenty-five years. Deborah owns and operates her own, private preschool where she teaches children between the ages of three and five (prekindergarten). It is there that she observes and studies early learning in action and reflects on how young children learn best. As an avid believer that the early childhood years are critical years for school success, she also believes that young children learn best when given natural opportunities to explore and examine their world through play and hands-on experiences. Deborah believes that the most important gifts you can give your child are a love for learning and the confidence to try.

Deborah shares her daily classroom experiences and insights with teachers and parents from all over the world through her *Teach Preschool* blog. You can visit the *Teach Preschool* blog at *www.teachpreschool.org* or visit the *Teach Preschool* Facebook page at *www.facebook.com/teachpreschool*.